Foreword by
The Honorable Rev. Floyd H. Flake, D.Min.
Senior Pastor, The Greater Allen A.M.E. Cathedral of New York
U.S. Congressman, Retired

A World of Possibilities

Unleashing The Power Within You

By

Darrell Jackson Sr.

Bloomington, IN Milton Keynes, UK

authorHOUSE®

AuthorHouse™
1663 Liberty Drive, Suite 200
Bloomington, IN 47403
www.authorhouse.com
Phone: 1-800-839-8640

AuthorHouse™ UK Ltd.
500 Avebury Boulevard
Central Milton Keynes, MK9 2BE
www.authorhouse.co.uk
Phone: 08001974150

This book is a work of non-fiction. Unless otherwise noted, the author
and the publisher make no explicit guarantees as to the accuracy of
the information contained in this book and in some cases, names of
people and places have been altered to protect their privacy.

First published by AuthorHouse 2/21/2007

ISBN: 978-1-4259-5477-2 (sc)
ISBN: 978-1-4259-5478-9 (hc)

Library of Congress Control Number: 2006931974

Printed in the United States of America
Bloomington, Indiana

This book is printed on acid-free paper.

Unless otherwise indicated, Scripture quotations
are from the King James Version of the Bible.

Manuscript Editor : Dennis J. Smith

Jackson, Sr., Darrell
A World of Possibilities: Unleashing the Power Within You

Praise for *A World of Possibilities*

This engaging book, entitled *A World of Possibilities,* by Darrell Jackson, Sr., provides for its reader a (surefire) spiritual antidote to contemporary depression and an out-of-this-world guarantee on living a victorious life.

This book of meaningful messages, which highlight the pluralities of our possibilities is also a book that is presented as a life-enhancing tapestry that is interwoven with the golden thread of dynamic faith in God.

When you have finished reading the first three chapters, you will already be convinced that God is the door, Faith is the key, the Bible (Word) is the source, and Possibilities are unlimited in that combination.

Another significant accomplishment of the book, *A World of Possibilities* was the extent to which these extraordinary possibilities were applied to the people of the world today.

The author of this book on "Possibilities," Darrell Jackson, Sr., is a serious student of the scripture and preacher of the Gospel, who has the talented ability to proclaim the scripture and to make it real and relevant to life in the twenty-first century. So in this book, you have "a world of possibilities" for "a world of disabilities"!

Finally, to properly appreciate this book, *A World of Possibilities,* one needs to understand that this book began before Jackson decided to write it. It began with his father and mother.

To know the author's mother, Mrs. Jannie Ruth (Lumpkin) Jackson, is to know a remarkable woman whose faith, intellect, compassion, insight, and positive thinking formed an unusual legacy, which she passed on to this author and to all of her children.

To have known the author's father, Bishop Andrew C. Jackson, is to have known one of today's most unusual men of God. He rose from material modesty to ecclesiastical greatness, but never lost the common touch. His life was that of an achiever with a reach for excellence as a pastor, a preacher, a builder, an innovator, a leader, a friend, and much more.

Jackson and his siblings were born to parents who believed in God and *A World of Possibilities*.

The author is the popular pastor of one of the mega-churches of Columbia and South Carolina, and his church is growing weekly. I refer to the Bible Way Church of Atlas Road. Visit this church on Sunday or any other day and you will experience profound possibilities in updated ministry.

Darrell Jackson, Sr., is also one of the strong and effective state senators of the state of South Carolina.

Read this book, *A World of Possibilities* and be prepared to deal with the comforting contagion that comes from a man who, himself, is on a superhighway to *A World of Possibilities*.

Bishop Frederick Calhoun James (Retired)
The African Methodist Episcopal Church

FOREWORD

A World of Possibilities challenges the reader to move with purpose into the realm of unlimited possibilities. The author properly notes that purpose is the launching pad on which you conceive your possibilities - the place where you dream about what life has in store for you, and create a design for success.

You know that there are challenges to be faced; yet it is purpose that propels you to heights unknown. As you reach one level of success after another, there comes a stage of realization that, "I can (indeed) do all things through Him who strengthens me."[1]

As you make your way through the terrain, the challenges, hardships, fears, loneliness, and other variables, you wonder if it's a worthwhile effort; but because you have purpose, you still see possibilities; thus, there is hope for success. Therefore, you continue in your pursuit, because you know that, "you have capacity to get beyond your past and go higher in your life."

These are times when, like the disciple Peter, you get sidetracked or lose sight of your purpose, but then God appears in the person of the Holy Spirit and brings clarity to your purpose for being. You are reminded of who you are, your purpose in life, and the unlimited possibilities that are inherent in the promises that are definitive of your future. Jackson says, "Don't let others push your buttons. Put these promises on the wall, the door is open." Then, he asks, "Are you willing to walk through it?"

All of us know someone who has loads of possibilities that have not been fully explored, and thus have not been realized. One of the worst things in life is to live and die without even reaching for the promise of purpose and possibility. Sometimes it's because of the negative voices from within, while at other times, it is from the voices of others. Moses, David, Job, and Joseph, the father of Jesus, are sterling examples of people who had to overcome inner voices and outward opinions.

Possibilities become broken dreams, nightmares, and "would've, could've, should've" testimonials when you fail to act in accordance with God's will and purpose for your life. So, what are you waiting for? Why are you still on the launching pad? Are you afraid of the challenges, the unexplained dark regions, or are you experiencing the fear of failure? Read, *A World of Possibilities*, then strap in and get ready for the ride of your life; the ride from purpose to the fulfillment of possibilities and the attainment of the goals that are synonymous with your purpose in life.

The Honorable Rev. Floyd H. Flake
Senior Pastor, The Greater Allen A.M.E.
Cathedral of New York
President, Wilberforce University
U.S. Congressman, (Retired)

DEDICATION

This book is dedicated in loving memory of my father, Bishop Andrew C. Jackson. My mentor, my teacher, my friend – you've been a source of inspiration on past accomplishments and will continue to be my motivation for future goals and dreams as I accept the challenge to move forward on the path God has set for me. You will live forever in my heart!

Your loving son, Darrell

Bishop Andrew C. Jackson
1927-2006

"I will not kick down any door but will walk through every door that God opens."

–Bishop A.C. Jackson

ACKNOWLEDGMENTS

For they refreshed my spirit and yours;
Therefore acknowledge such…

1 Corinthians 16:18, NKJV

It is both awesome and humbling to look back and see how the hand of God has brought me to the place where this book can be in your hands today.

Writing a book, especially one that focuses on developing individuals spiritually, is a major undertaking. Along the road, one must seek the guidance and support of others in an attempt to present the best of what one has to offer.

I am blessed to have had the love, support, and assistance of many wonderful and talented people. There are really no words that can acknowledge my appreciation of your support. While I cannot list you all, I owe my deepest and heartfelt thanks to a few people in particular.

My greatest asset is my family. From the very beginning, my wife, Willie Mae, has been a supporter in all that God has given me to do. And thanks go to my wonderful sons, Darrell Jr. and Antoine Joseph.

I would like to acknowledge my mother, Jannie R. (Lumpkin) Jackson and the late Bishop Andrew C. Jackson, whose lives of absolute devotion to Jesus Christ was the guiding light of my life. God placed in their hands the chisel that has shaped every aspect of my life.

I would be remiss if I did not acknowledge with thanks and appreciation the members of Bible Way Church of Atlas Road, whose love and prayers have sustained me.

Janice Cohen, thank you for administering this project. Your skills were essential to this process. To Beverly Dozier, Nicole Holland, Dennis Smith, and Calvin W. Jackson, thank you for editing and reviewing this book. I want to thank Andrea McCoy, my executive assistant, for putting together the sermon notes. I am also grateful to Joseph L. Jackson, (my uncle) whose words of encouragement inspire me to always pursue excellence.

However, while my thanks to those named above remains boundless, responsibility for the final outcome is mine alone, by the grace of God.

CONTENTS

Part Three

Part Four

INTRODUCTION

Reading *The Power of Focus* by Jack Canfield, Mark Victor Hansen, and Les Hewitt blessed me in my personal life. The authors discuss the value of focusing, specifically, how to focus on concepts long enough to digest them.[1] I am one who will start one book, and set it aside and start another book, setting that aside to start yet another. By the end of the year, I may have half-read five or six books, and not have totally digested any of them. The Lord took me to a spiritual level that I did not even think was possible as He began to focus my attention. I read, studied, and prayed about the dynamics of *The Power of Focus*. God allowed me to master the concept of focusing until it was a part of my subconscious. There came a point in my life that when I needed to pray, the dynamics of focus became a part of my spirit, a part of my prayer life, and a part of my walk with the Lord. As I found myself saying the things that I had digested, and achieving the things I expected, I discovered *A World of Possibilities*.

As this book opens up *A World of Possibilities* to you, it is important for you to know that it is possible to have what you expect. Sometimes we live our lives believing that we are not worthy of the blessings of God. The enemy plays psychological tricks on us, and he would have us doubting ourselves. We become depressed over what we haven't achieved and what we do not have. We are, too often, our own worst critics. We need to learn to rebuke that spirit that says you can't and remember you can have "exceeding abundantly more that you can ask or think."[2]

Many of you are on the verge of greatness. All you need to do is to walk through the door of opportunity, which leads to a world of possibilities. Dreams you may have put on the shelf of life are possible to achieve. By applying the concepts of this book, you will eliminate boundaries placed on your life by doubt.

Hopefully this book will encourage you to stop worrying about things that may have gone wrong in your life and to focus now on those things that are possible. Take your dreams from the shelf and dust them off, with hope, positioning yourself to enter into a world of possibilities.

CHAPTER ONE

From Purpose to Possibilities

I know thy works: behold, I have set before thee an open door, and no man can shut it: for thou hast a little strength, and hast kept my word, and hast not denied my name.

Revelation 3:8

Jesus said unto him, If thou canst believe, all things [are] possible to him that believeth.

Mark 9:23

Our purpose in life determines our possibilities in life. Possibilities must follow purpose. God will not give you possibilities if you cannot understand purpose. If He did, you would not know what to do with the possibilities that you have been afforded. I have often seen people on the verge of greatness and they did not even know it. In fact, they would not recognize a blessing if it were right in their faces. When you understand your purpose in life, your possibilities become clear. You begin to understand why you had to lose that job in order to go to the next job. You begin to understand why you had to leave and someone else had to come in. You begin to

1

understand why you had to go through what you went through for all those years.

Even before you ask God to make clear the possibilities for your life, make sure you understand your purpose in life. Too often, we erroneously equate our purpose in life with elevated celebrations of accomplishments, which bring us personal recognition. It is not important that others know what you do; that's a spirit that we all must keep under control. There are times in all our lives in which we feel unappreciated, as if others don't understand what we are doing or how hard we are working or what we are going through. Does it really matter if people don't understand? Does it really matter if no one comes up to you and says, "Gosh, you're wonderful" if you know that you are touching lives? That platform mentality can be devastating. I often remember my late father, Bishop Andrew C. Jackson, saying, "Sometimes the adversary will allow elevation to do more harm to you than deflation." When some people lose their material wealth, they pray harder than ever before. When others walk out on them, they come to church more than ever before. On the other hand, when you are elevated and things are going well in your life, you are making more money than you've ever made before, and everyone is now calling you because they want to be your friend, then that is the time to lean on God. Not everyone can handle being blessed. But when you understand your purpose in life, you can say, "Now I see my possibilities." Possibilities cannot happen without purpose.

Possibilities derive from the word "possible," which means "being within limits of ability, capacity, or realization."[1] It is that thing which is within reach. Those who say, "I can't do it" are not living within the possibilities that God has given them. It is within your ability to be blessed. You have the capacity to get beyond your past and go higher in your life. You should realize that where you are headed is greater than where you come from. If you don't believe that, stop reading now, because everything in this book will be meaningless theological babble. You've got to believe it for yourself. I have seen too many scripture-quoting people lacking confidence. The reason they have not ventured out is because they are afraid. Perfect love casts out all fear.[2]

Simon Peter may have had a big mouth and been a violent person, but when he was on a boat looking at what appeared to be Jesus standing on the water, Peter had enough courage to say, "Lord, just give me a word. I can't see your face, but if I hear your voice, I'll recognize that and I'll come out." To which Jesus said, "Come." [3] Note that Jesus did not say, "You come only, Peter." He just said, "Come." Anyone who heard that word could have left the boat.

God is speaking the same word to you that he is speaking to everyone else. The problem is that you don't have enough faith and courage to leave the boat and step out into the world of possibilities. As with Peter, you may run into a hitch, and while you are out there, you may start to sink. At that time, remember who invited you to come. Because Jesus invited Peter to come, he reached forth his hand and saved Peter when he was about to fall.[4] When Jesus went back to glory, he needed to leave one person in charge. He did not leave his best friend, John, in charge. Perhaps he knew that if the boat got rocky and the waves got rough, John would be too cautious, too conservative, and too reserved to leave the boat. He entrusted the care of his mother to John but not the care of his ministry. When he needed to leave someone in charge of his ministry, he went to the very man who had denied him on the night of his betrayal, the man who had cursed out the girl, saying, "Woman, I don't know Him." [5] Jesus knew that Peter would leave the boat. Jesus needed someone like Peter who said, "I'll never leave you; I'll never forsake you; don't wash my feet!" Others would think it, but wouldn't say it. Jesus needed someone with courage and strength to walk into possibilities. On the morning of the resurrection, Jesus told the women at the tomb to go tell his disciples and Peter to meet him in Galilee.[6] Perhaps the only one he called by name was Peter because Peter left the boat.

You may be living in worse conditions than ever before because you aren't willing to leave the boat. You won't take any chances because you've got to see your way through everything. Faith is not seeing your way through. Faith is the substance of things hoped for, the evidence of things not seen.[7] If you have to see it, it's not faith. You've got to be willing to walk out on nothing and believe that something will be there before your feet hit the ground. You've got to have enough faith to step out. That is why purpose and possibilities work together. God will only present us with possibilities that fit our purpose. Don't try to compare what God offered Peter to what God offered Paul. They have two separate purposes within the kingdom of God. Likewise, God will give you possibilities that fit your purpose.

In the book of Revelation, God speaks to seven churches. There are occasions when he says the same things to many of the churches. There are also instances where he makes very specific promises to very specific churches. There is a church in Philadelphia in which God gives a specific word: *"Behold, I have set before you an open door that no one can shut."* [8] This is not said to the Laodiceans or to the church in Smyrna, but to the church in Philadelphia because that church's purpose fit that possibility. God was giving this church an awesome opportunity to do something fantastic. He opened a door for them that no one could shut. Notice what he does *not* say. He does not say, "I am going to push you through the door" or "I am going to drag you through it." In order for them to get through it, they had to *walk* through it. That's where faith comes in. You have to have enough faith to walk through the door! One of the greatest tragedies in life is standing before a blessing and not even realizing it. God has given you an awesome opportunity. Will you walk through the door?

The church of Philadelphia was set apart from the others in several ways. They were lively. They were genuine and not pretentious. With this church, what you saw was what you got. It was all about a purpose and a mission for them. They were alive in their praise. Being alive in praise is not equated with how much noise you make. It is equated with the sincerity of your praise. When you worship God in spirit and in truth, you are sincere to the movement of God. When God chooses to bless people, He blesses those who are genuine. The church of Philadelphia was a church of faithful people.

If you are faithful to God, God will bless you as you've never been blessed before. He rewards them that diligently seek Him.[9] That implies faithfulness. You can't just hit and miss. You can't come to the first Sunday service of the year and not show up again until the next year, and call yourself faithful. Faithfulness is going through the roughest times in your life and holding fast to your integrity. Faithfulness is holding on in spite of circumstances. If you want a door of opportunity opened, become faithful. Faithfulness is not what others say about you; that's bragging. Faithfulness is what God says about you. Most of what you do will not be known by others – and you don't have to tell them about it. God knows about it. Harry Truman once said, "A man can accomplish a whole lot if he doesn't mind who gets the credit." [10] He spoke those words to his presidential cabinet. If your name never gets called, you should continue to do your best. You are not doing it for man, but to the glory of God. The Philadelphians were faithful to God.

Finally, the Philadelphians were loving people. They did not just show their love to God who loves freely and gives freely. They also showed their love to one another. Can you love the person who gets on your last nerve? Can you love the person who gives you headaches? Can you love the person who does not look like you? Can you love everyone, or is your love discriminating? Do you love people based on who they are, what they have, and what they can do for you? The Philadelphia church was blessed because they had an open-door policy. Historical writings on the book of Revelation reveal this open-door policy. Religious leaders of the time criticized the Philadelphia church because they let anyone through their doors. That meant if you walked in, you were welcomed and you were special, regardless of how rich or poor you were. Because they opened their doors, God opened His door by telling them that they could walk in and ask for what they wanted. When you have an attitude that loves everyone and you treat all people like they are significant, God will bless you. We all need to curse the spirit of selfishness that stems from our egos, which tells each of us that we deserve more than others. In doing so, you will receive a blessing and not even know how you got it because you have done nothing to receive your blessing.

God promised the Philadelphia church that He would open a door that no one could shut. Likewise, God is going to give you something that no one can take back from you. Aren't you glad to know that God is going to do something for you and that no one can hinder the blessings of God? When God gets ready to shower you with blessings, no one will be able to stand in your way! That is why it is impossible for others to block the blessings that God has for you. You can block them, but others cannot. It does not matter what others think or say. When the door is opened, no one can shut it. The Philadelphian church was harassed by the other churches that felt that members of the Philadelphian church were liberals who lacked complete theological background. The history of the churches of Asia Minor notes how the other churches looked down on the Philadelphian church, believing that "anything goes" in there. Anyone could come to the church in Philadelphia. God said to the Laodiceans that he would spew them out of his mouth because He did not even want to get next to them.[11] God despised the way they tasted. But to the church in Philadelphia, God promised to open a door that no one could shut. What an awesome promise!

Put it this way: God will make your enemies your footstool. Get ready to be blessed. God is going to make those who mistreated you fall down and worship at your feet. God can do it. He is working on a blessing for you right now. What should you do to your enemy? The Lord said, you have no need to fight this fight because the battle is not yours. It's the Lord's.[12] Put away your weapons; unclench your hands. You don't have to strike. You don't have to fight this fight. God will take care of your enemy. The worst place a person can be is between a blessed person and God. Don't worry what people say. If someone is mistreating you, don't worry about him or her because one day he or she will be at your feet.

So you didn't get what you asked for last year, and you've wanted it for the last five years, but because of your patience and because you've kept God's word, God is going to keep from you the hour of temptation (the hour of tribulation). What others go through, you won't have to go through because you've been faithful. God has set before you an open door. Now, it's up to you to walk through it. Continue to be faithful and let patience have its perfect work in you.

Don't let others push your buttons. Put these promises on your wall. The door is open. Are you willing to walk through it? Are you willing to do whatever God asks you to do to walk in divine possibilities? All things are possible if you just believe.

CHAPTER TWO

Who Me? The People of Possibilities

And Moses answered and said, but, behold, they will not believe me, nor hearken unto my voice: for they will say, The Lord hath not appeared unto thee.

Exodus 4:1

And he said unto him, Oh my Lord, wherewith shall I save Israel? Behold, my family is poor in Manasseh, and I am the least in my father's house. And the Lord said unto him, Surely I will be with thee, and thou shalt smite the Midianites as one man.

Judges 6:15-16

Now when Jesus was risen early the first day of the week, he appeared first to Mary Magdalene, out of whom he had cast seven devils.

Mark 16:9

It is a wonderful thing to understand the possibilities of your potential. One of the worst things in the world is a person who does not live up to his or her potential. Some people are stuck in mediocrity. They are happy being average. They don't want to excel or to exceed; they don't want to go anywhere.

10

I've noticed that most people rooted in prejudice have a lack of exposure. Some people's minds are so restricted that they think everyone in the world should look like them, think like them, act like them, and live the way they do. Those who travel are more exposed to other cultures than those who have not traveled. I believe that it is God's desire to expose us to a lot more than we are used to. In other words, get ready to go higher and deeper in the Lord. Some people won't walk into possibilities because they can't deal with the unknown. They have to deal with what they can touch and see. They can't walk out on faith.

If you have felt that you could not do it, that you can't walk out on faith, I want you to know that you can do it. God wants to expand your horizon. You can start that business, you can get that job, and you can buy that home. Even if you now find yourself alone, you can still make it. God may have allowed the situation in order to elevate you. Sometimes you've got to do what is called pruning. The problem with pruning is that it doesn't look good when it is first done, but there is a purpose for the separation. When you prune a bush or tree in the winter, it may look skinny and sickly, but in the spring, you will see that the bush or tree looks better than it ever has. Sometimes, in order to acquire things in life, you have to give up some things. You may be going through the pruning process in your life, during which God has taken away some of your personal things and has taken away people who you were very close to. Now, it doesn't look as if you are going to be successful, but looks do not matter because as believers in Christ, we are not walking by sight, we are walking by faith.

You do not have to be perfect in order for God to bless you and to use you. You may think that you are not deserving of a blessing because you are less than perfect. If God marked iniquity, who would stand?[1] It is always the intent of the adversary to make you doubt your credentials and doubt your position in life to receive the blessings of God. God has never expected perfection to be a prerequisite for your use in the Kingdom of God. This chapter takes a look through the Holy Scriptures to identify some of the people of possibilities whom God used. Consider the first man, Adam, and his disobedience to God. Consider Noah, the one whom God used to save a people to replenish the earth, and how he was drunk. Noah did this and more while he was still on the Ark, but it did not disqualify him from being used by God. God chose Noah even before he "messed up." [2] God, knowing what Noah had done, still included him in the "Hall of Faith" when he talked about the patriarchs of old. From the beginning to the end of the Bible, all the people whom God used had weaknesses in their lives.

Moses was a man with no confidence, yet God chose him to lead a whole generation of people. God did not tell Moses to lead people who did not know anything about him into a land of liberty and prosperity. Some of the toughest people you can ever have authority over are the people who know you. It is sometimes better to lead people who do not know you.

Have you ever been promoted to a supervisor's job and had to supervise those with whom you used to work? You haven't "caught it" until you "catch it" from people who tell you that you used to be where they are. It is hard to lead people who were your equals or people who do not think much of you. Moses was given the difficult situation of going back to where he came from, to lead people who did not like him from the beginning. God could have chosen anyone. He did not have to find Moses who was tending his father-in-law's sheep. God could have gotten someone else. He could have sent some angelic force to lead the people out of captivity, but I imagine God saying, "Moses, I want you. I know that you were an orphan, thinking that your mother abandoned you. I know that you were raised by the enemy, eating his food and wearing his clothes." Moses did not look like the people whom God told him to lead, and if that was not bad enough, Moses had murdered an Egyptian. The problem is, we often worry about the people we are sent to help, and we often forget that it was God who sent us. You've got to remember who anointed you to go and do it.

God has ushered in a transformation in your life. You are more dynamic than you think you are, but you have not yet confessed the changes that God has created in your life. Moses was not an eloquent speaker before he witnessed the burning bush, nor was he afterward. He told the Lord that he was of slow speech. He could not believe that the Lord was calling him to go back and issue a word to Pharaoh and to millions of people who were in bondage. Moses felt that God should have chosen someone more charismatic.

"And the Lord said unto him, who hath made man's mouth? Or who maketh the dumb, or deaf, or the seeing, or the blind? Have not I the Lord? Now therefore go, and I will be with thy mouth, and teach thee what thou shalt say." [3]

Some of us are not chosen by God because we have not allowed Him to teach us. We think we know everything. God can only use those who have room for expansion. As smart as you are, God cannot use you when you believe that you already know everything. You believe that you are smarter than anyone else is. You think that you should be God. You talk back to God, telling him what to do, telling Him what He hasn't done right. You have no room for expansion. Don't ever get caught up in who you are. The worst thing that a person who works for the Kingdom can do is to be overconfident. God does not need any cocky, prima donna people who think that all they need is one chance and the whole world will bow at their feet. You are going to die broke, busted, and disgusted *with* all your gifts and callings. There is nothing worse than seeing someone gifted and not using their gift because he or she does not have the right attitude about God who gave the gift.

When the angel of the Lord appeared to Gideon, he was hiding behind a winepress. Gideon was trying not to be seen, heard, or noticed. He did not want any attention; he was very content with being mediocre, and if God had not changed his life, he would have died hiding from the enemy. When Gideon allowed God to use him, he became known as a mighty man of valor, a mighty man of courage, a mighty man of war. Gideon had not previously been to any wars. He had not fought one battle. He had not done one courageous thing in his entire life when God spoke to him. When God told Gideon that he was a mighty man of valor, Gideon turned around...

"And he said unto him, Oh my Lord, wherewith shall I save Israel? Behold, my family is poor in Manasseh, and I am the least in my father's house. And the Lord said unto him, Surely I will be with thee, and thou shalt smite the Midianites as one man." [4]

In other words, when God gets ready to use you, you don't need any help. Even though He reduced the army that Gideon would lead to 300 warriors, Gideon still didn't need that many. God had already said that Gideon would smite the enemy as one man.

Have you been hiding from God? Have you been hiding from your gifts, your calling, and the anointing that God has on you? Has God told you to go somewhere, to do something, and to venture out on faith, but you are hiding because you are waiting on just *one more sign?* How many more signs do you need? An evil generation seeks signs! You don't need signs; you need a word from God, and if you've got a word from God, why do you need a sign? Why does God have to show you anything if God has already told you something? If God has spoken a word to you about you, why do you need others to confirm it? Are you waiting for others to pat you on the back and confirm it and say, "Go ahead"? They may not ever do that. Some of these people you look to for encouragement know that you are being used by God.

Since they are caught up in their own jealousy, don't expect them to encourage you. If you are waiting for others to encourage you, you may just die without ever getting what you wanted. Start paying attention to how you praise and encourage others in your life. Give people you care about their flowers while they can still smell them. God doesn't always speak a word about who you are right now. Sometimes, God speaks a word about who you are about to become. If you don't understand faith-speaking, you don't think that God is speaking to you. Don't get stuck on where you used to be. You need to hear a word from God about where you are going. When God speaks to you about your situation, He is telling you that you are more than a conqueror. You are more than someone who has to depend on others just to get your breakthrough. God has given you more than enough. Many of you today are waiting for someone to go places with you, thinking that you need a ministry partner. If God called you, you can do it all by yourself, because God and you make a majority, and if God be for you, who can be against you? Who are you waiting for? God spoke a word to Gideon before the army had even been formed. If God walks with you daily, does it really matter if other people don't accept you in their social circles? Have enough confidence to know that God has told you what to do. You don't need confirmation from any member or from the pastor. They may not get it right as it relates to your life, but when you know that God has instructed you, you should move forward. This doesn't mean that you should not be obedient to leadership. You are not a lone ranger. One thing that God does not do is use someone with a haughty spirit.

According to scripture, seven demons came out of Mary Magdalene. She was unstable. You would not have wanted her, but God looked beyond where she was and saw where she was going to be. Many of us have had more than seven demons, we've had legions of demons, and God still uses us.

No one followed Jesus without being invited to follow Him. He said to his disciples, *"Come follow me."* Jesus was very selective about the people who would be in His inner circle. If, after Jesus had delivered Mary Magdalene from those seven demons, he had invited her to His inner circle by saying to her, "Come on, be one of my disciples, be one of my followers, I want you to walk with me," you've got to believe that one of those chauvinistic men who was walking with Jesus would have said to Jesus, "Come here, let me pull you to the side. I know that you mean well, and there might be something that she can do in Galilee, but I don't think that you want her to be a part of your inner circle because she has a reputation. I know you delivered her, but can't you leave her at home?" Thank God, He looked beyond her faults just to see her needs. As with Mary Magdalene, aren't you glad to know that God doesn't check with others before he appoints and anoints you? If God checked with others, it's doubtful that you would have been chosen by Him.

While Jesus was hanging between two thieves, eleven out of his twelve male disciples had deserted Him. Mary Magdalene understood, however, that if you have lived with and been delivered from seven demons, you are not afraid of anything else. The issue with disciples Thomas, James, and Peter was that they had not been delivered from much. They were still fearful. God likes those who have come through difficulties, because their allegiance is with their deliverer. The reason that Mary Magdalene stood at the foot of the Cross and kneeled down is because she appreciated that Jesus had delivered her from so much. She could have looked that Roman soldier in his face and said, "There isn't a thing that you can do to me that hasn't already been done to me."

Mary Magdalene had to be at the Cross. She could not be anywhere else. She wasn't privileged to be a tax collector or a physician. She wasn't a fisherman. She was a woman who was demonically possessed, and Jesus had saved her life. On that resurrection morning, He appeared *first* to Mary Magdalene. He didn't appear to Peter, James, or John; He didn't even appear to His mother first. He went to this woman first. The first one ever to preach the resurrection message was a reformed woman who had issues. The first evangelist of the New Testament was a woman called Mary Magdalene — out of whom seven demons came. Don't let people tell you that God can't use you.

There are seven things that everyone who is used by God has in common:

1. All have issues. If you've never had an issue, then you are not qualified to be used by God. God uses those who have gone through something significant.

2. They do not seek position or recognition. They did not go out to create it for themselves. God's anointing will find you...*these blessings shall overtake you.*[5] You don't have to sit around waiting. You don't have to reach back and grab it. Just keep going, and the blessings will catch up with you and overtake you. Don't change your faithfulness.

3. Others would not choose them. If you have been rejected by men, you are just right to be used by God. God likes to use those whom others think can't do it.

4. Past struggles complement current assignments. The past struggles, all the trials you've ever gone through, all the heartaches, all the broken relationships, and all the hospital stays, etc., will all complement what God has planned for you. You had to go through it. Every

19

struggle that you have gone through will complement the position in which God is going to use you. God is going to use your struggles so you can bless someone else.

5. They obey the voice of God.

6. They are willing to follow God all the way.

7. They always give God the credit for their success.

Reflect on what God has already done in your life. Apply these seven commonalities to your life. Ask yourself if you are willing to give God the credit and the glory. Are you willing to follow God all the way? Or will you quit on God? Those who haven't been through a struggle are more likely to quit on God. You may be going through struggles, but God says that they are necessary for your future assignment. Heartaches are necessary for your future assignment. You do not know it yet, but there is something that you are destined to do. The struggles in your life will complement your assignment. God knows what you have gone through. He has seen your struggles and your heartaches, and still he wants you. Are you going to follow Him? You must make a personal commitment to Him. When you do that, circumstances will begin to change. Our destiny is oftentimes shaped by the unknown. We don't always know why God allows us to go through it, but in the end, He will make His will clear, and you will understand. You deserve to be blessed. God will protect you when others cannot. When you are destined to be used by God, your steps are ordered by the Lord, and though you stumble, you will not be destroyed.

CHAPTER THREE

The Promises of Possibilities

And it shall come to pass, if thou shalt hearken diligently unto the voice of the Lord thy God, to observe and to do all his commandments which I command thee this day, that the Lord thy God will set thee on high above all nations of the earth: And all these blessings shall come on thee, and overtake thee, if thou shalt hearken unto the voice of the Lord thy God. Blessed shalt thou be in the city, and blessed shalt thou be in the field...

Deuteronomy 28:1-3

People of possibilities are the ones who have the promises of possibilities. They are the ones with an assurance that God will do miraculous things in their lives. Although a nation came out of Egypt and died in the wilderness, a new nation emerged out of the wilderness experience. What many do not realize is that only two of those who left Egypt actually went into the land of Canaan: Joshua and Caleb. All the others died in the wilderness because of their unbelief. God had delivered them through mighty acts; He fed them manna from heaven; He gave them meat. God even gave them water from a rock, yet these people doubted whether God could protect them in transition. God was tired of them. They had not turned their backs on

Moses. They turned their backs on God. God allowed them to wander in the wilderness for forty years.

The difference between a journey and a wandering trip is *purpose.* The Jews left Egypt but lost their focus and their purpose. It ceased being a journey and became a wandering experience for them. Many of us find ourselves at times wandering because we lose focus. We lose direction. We lose purpose. Even Moses would not enter into the Promised Land, because he allowed the people he was leading to make him lose his promise of possibilities. Don't allow those around you to make you lose what you are entitled to have. You've got to learn how to separate yourself from people who want to bring you down. All the Jews who followed Moses died in the wilderness except Joshua and Caleb. What made these two unusual is that they stood up and saw the same things that everyone else saw, but said, "We are well able to possess the land." [1] The author expounds on the promises for obedience and the curses for disobedience. God makes promises of blessings, but He also makes promises of curses and destruction. A promise is worth as much as anything in life that you can get. In other words, there is nothing more comforting in life than to have the promises of God concerning your possibilities. The doors of possibilities are what God says He will open. *"Behold I set before you an open door that no one will be able to shut."* [2] What more can you ask for? God has put you in a position to be so blessed that you do not have to make a door, neither do you have to keep it open. All you have to do is walk through it. God has provided opportunities for you.

God will keep His promise. He has promised you a good thing, and the day will come when He will perform it. He will do what He has promised. If you haven't gotten it yet, just hold on. It has to be on its way because the promises of God in Him are Yea, and in Him Amen.[3] You don't need a second opinion on God's Word. You don't need three or four to touch and agree on God's Word. You can touch and agree on being *faithful* to His Word. If His Word says for you to do something, there is nothing to touch and agree on. Simon Peter says, *"Whereby are given unto us exceeding great and precious promises…."*[4] You have been given precious promises. This is not an ordinary promise. A promise is only as good as the word of the person who promises to do it. You may have received promises from someone who says things to you that really make you feel good at the time, but these promises don't really change your destiny, because you know this person is not going to keep his or her word. All you have are sounding brass and tinkling symbols. But when God makes a promise, God stands behind His Word. God is the promise maker and the promise keeper. He will do just what He says He will do. It doesn't matter what happens in your life. God will keep His promises. God will be faithful to His promises. The problem is that we don't often realize what we have. We have blessings waiting for us that we don't even know about. You may have something that God has given you that does not look like anything to other people. Guess what? It's not their blessing. It's your blessing. You should be proud of what God has for you.

Whatever God blesses you with thank Him for it. Your car may not have air conditioning, but roll your window down and wave at people and say, *"at least it's mine."* You are a lot better off driving your broken-down car than those who are driving fancy cars and deep in debt. Learn how to be grateful for what God has blessed you with. Be careful not to envy the grass on the other side of the track. It is not always as green as it looks. Sometimes it's not even grass. Sometimes it's Astroturf!

I don't compare my blessings with those of others. I have seen people get into comparing the sizes of churches. What difference does that make? God was good when our church was on a storefront on Bluff Road. We are just now seeing the manifestation of God's blessings. We praised God when we didn't have anything. We continued to praise Him after we moved to a larger church. I don't have historical amnesia. I remember from where God has brought our church. Never forget from where God has brought you.

The promises of God are not automatic. The promises of God are conditional. He says, *"And it shall come to pass, if thou shalt hearken diligently unto the voice of the Lord thy God, to observe [and] to do all his commandments which I command thee."* [5] In other words, there is a condition for your possibilities, and if you do not meet those conditions, you can jump and wave your hands and say whatever declarations your pastor wants you to say, but you won't get a thing until you meet the criteria that God expects out of your life. God is not looking for perfection. He is looking for faithfulness. God is looking for those who can get knocked down and turned around and get up again for the Lord. When you can diligently hear the voice of God and do what He has asked you to do and observe His commandments and hear His Word, the blessings will be so magnificent that you won't be able to count them!

If you hearken diligently to the voice of the Lord, then you can expect to be blessed. That's what God says. Consider the parable about the two houses; one built on sand and the other on a solid foundation. Both houses were perfect until a storm came. Similarly, you really never know the sterner stuff of which you are made until you go through some things. When we were building our worship center, we were told that we wouldn't know if the builders did a good job on our roof until we got a hard rain. After the first hard rain, I called to find out if there was a leak. I was told that there was one small leak. I had my assistant call the company back to come fix it. That was something to consider. You really don't know how saved you are until you go through a storm. Have you ever gone through a storm? You may be living in sunshine right now, but your test will be through the storm. Your test may be when someone leaves you financially broke, or your test may be when you are in a doctor's office and your results come back positive, and the doctor says that he has difficult news to give you. The enemy will say to you "Praise God now!" You should put the enemy on hold and say, "I will bless the Lord at all times." Whatever storm comes, you should praise God. Can you praise God in the midst of a difficult situation? Can you praise God when you don't know how you are going to make ends meet? Have you ever had bad news with trouble all around you, but it did not impact your praise? Those who knew you did not know what was going on in your life until it was over because your disposition never changed. It did not impact your praise. You should not be able to look at a person and tell what he or she is going through. You should be able to stand firm under adversities. People should look at you and say, "Something good must have happened to you." Just tell them, "All is well." Sometimes you have to speak into existence what you know the possibilities are concerning you.

Five possibilities of blessings that God has for us:

God will exalt them above all other nations and it shall come to pass if thou shall hearken diligently to the voice of the Lord thy God and to observe and do all the commandments which I have commanded thee this day, that the Lord shall set thee on high above all nations of the earth.[6]

1. God is about to bless you and there isn't a thing that the enemy can do about it. The difference between exaltation by God and one by man is this: When man exalts you, every now and then, he wants to bring you back down. Man will say, "I made you and I can bring you down; I

27

gave it to you, I can take it from you." When God exalts you, however, there isn't anything that man can do about your heavenly promotion. That's why you have to remain patient. You have been celebrating what is not real. Wait until God drops the real thing in your life! When God sets you up, His word declares, *"I will set thee on high above all the nations of the earth."* [7] The challenge is that you want to be like others, and God wants you to be above others. You can't have the attitude that says, "If I can be like so-and-so..." Don't try to be like anyone else. Be better. Set yourself apart and allow God to set you up above all the other nations. When God exalts you, it is not so that you can be complacent with mediocrity. God exalts you so that you can expect excellence. Don't get happy with mediocrity.

2. The blessings of God shall do two things: come upon you and overtake you. If you hearken unto the voice of the Lord, you won't have to pursue your blessings. Your blessings will pursue you. In other words, you won't have to chase behind good things. Good things will chase behind you. You won't have to strive and connive to trick people to get what you think should be yours. What is yours will find you. The difference is that God will not reward you because of your pursuit. God will reward you because of your faithfulness. God says that blessings shall come upon you. How often have the

best things in life that happened to you been the things that you were not even looking for? Have you ever been offered a job that you were not even looking for? You were not thinking about the job, and someone walked up to you and asked if you were interested in it. What about the house you never thought you would live in? You were looking in the wrong places in your search for a house. God wanted you to go to the better side of town to own a house. God does not want you to rent; he wants you to own your house. The blessings of God and the promises of God are Yea and in Him, Amen.[8] These blessings have already been established. You don't have to pursue blessings. The problem is that we've wasted all our spiritual lives chasing blessings. Wait until God blesses you. God will open up the windows of heaven and pour you out a blessing. I am not saying to become complacent. I am saying, *"They that wait upon the Lord shall renew their strength."* [9] There is virtue in waiting and allowing God's blessings to come upon you. Even if you have to walk down the road before you get a blessing, walk knowing that, eventually, what you had been promised is going to catch up with you. You may not see it now; you may not realize it now, but it's not the end yet. *Your destiny has not been fulfilled until your promises have been realized.* That is to say, if you don't have it yet, and you remain faithful to the Lord, it is on its way. You should thank God for the process. If God has said it about you, God is going to do just what He said.

3. You will be blessed no matter where you are: in the city or in the field. It is not your location that matters, but your promise. It really doesn't matter where you are. What matters is what has been said about you. Some people are confused, thinking that they should be further along and that they should have more, but it is not about your place; it's about your promise. God can bless you regardless of your place. You are blessed in the city and blessed in the field. This concept stems from a time when those who worked in the city were considered affluent. Those in the field were considered "have-nots." People looked down on those who worked in the field. Even during the antebellum period, the days of slavery and reconstruction, there were all categories of people: house slaves and field slaves. There was a strong distinction between the two. The greatest threat that a master had over house slaves is that he would put them back in the field. Once a slave worked in the house, he never wanted to go back to the field. Nat Turner's rebellion failed because one of his own turned him in. That person probably had a perception that his place in life mattered more than anything else did. It is not about your circumstance; it's about your promise. I've got the promises of God that can't be taken away. If you learn

how to praise God now for your promises, God will bless you. In other words, you don't have to wait until you get to a new place in order to praise God. You can praise God about your future from where you are now. As broke as you are, you can still praise God. As sick as you are, as lonely as you are, you can still praise God. You may have been waiting for your situation to change, but you can still praise God. All you need God to say is, "By my stripes, you can be healed." Thank God for the promises that are in Him Yea and in Him, Amen.

"And the LORD shall make thee plenteous in goods, in the fruit of thy body, and in the fruit of thy cattle, and in the fruit of thy ground, in the land which the LORD sware unto thy fathers to give thee." [10]

4. The Lord will give you more than enough. Stop asking for provision and ask for abundance. Provision means that you have paid your bills. Abundance means that you had enough to pay your bills, put some in the bank, and go out to eat dinner. I have stopped praying just for provision. I don't have to say, "Lord, just give me enough to barely get by." That's not my prayer. God said in His Word that He would open the windows of heaven and pour me out a blessing that there will not be room enough to receive it.[11] Don't settle for provision. Ask for abundance so that you can save some, so that you can give some away and be a blessing to someone else. There is a parable in the New Testament about a rich man who

thought within himself, saying, *"What shall I do, because I have no room where to bestow my fruits? And he said, This will I do: I will pull down my barns, and build greater; and there will I bestow all my fruits and my goods. And I will say to my soul, Soul, thou hast much goods laid up for many years; take thine ease, eat, drink, and be merry. But God said unto him, Thou fool, this night thy soul shall be required of thee: then whose shall those things be, which thou hast provided?"* [12]

Evangelist and author Tommy Tenney dealt with this issue in his book, *The God Chasers*.[13] The issue in this parable wasn't the two barns. The issue was that the man's head was too full. God doesn't mind your barns being full, as long as your ego is down. When the man said in that parable, *"I will say to my soul...take thine ease, eat, drink and be merry,"* [14] that's where he erred. Don't let the enemy fool you into believing that God does not want you to have abundance. God wants you to have abundance, but God wants you to stay humble in your abundance and to acknowledge where your abundance came from. God wants you to dress in nice clothes and ride in fine cars and for you to have money in the bank and enjoy life and to leave an inheritance, but also God wants you to fall on your knees, saying, "Thank you, Lord, I never knew that I would be able to do something like this." Can you praise God for prosperity? Praise God for bringing you a mighty long way!

5. *The Lord shall open unto thee His good treasure.* You don't have to wait for the treasures of men. God is going to

open up his bank account, and when God writes you a check, it won't bounce!

Now you know what you are entitled to have. Go possess your promises. It doesn't matter what others think when God has given you a promise. Remember, the promises of God are not automatic. If you diligently hearken unto the voice of the Lord and do his commandments, these blessings will come upon you and overtake you.

CHAPTER FOUR

The Enemies of Possibilities

And the same day, when the even was come, he saith unto them, Let us pass over unto the other side. And when they had sent away the multitude, they took him even as he was in the ship. And there were also with him other little ships. And there arose a great storm of wind, and the waves beat into the ship, so that it was now full. And he was in the hinder part of the ship, asleep on a pillow: and they awake him, and say unto him, Master, carest thou not that we perish? And he arose, and rebuked the wind, and said unto the sea, Peace, be still. And the wind ceased, and there was a great calm. And he said unto them, Why are ye so fearful? how is it that ye have no faith? And they feared exceedingly, and said one to another, What manner of man is this, that even the wind and the sea obey him?

Mark 4:35 – 41

Do you realize that for every possibility of your life, there is an enemy trying to keep you from obtaining the possibilities and the promises that have been given to you? Without sounding pessimistic or negative, it is important for you to praise God not only for the promises, it is equally important for you to recognize the hindrances that prevent you from accepting the possibilities that are in your life.

34

We are people of possibilities because we have been given the promises of possibilities. Many people, however, go their entire lives without getting these promises or realizing these possibilities. Your possibilities are not automatic. They are not bestowed upon you without conditions.

In order for you to realize the possibilities that God has for you, there are some things that must be in place in your life. Consider the Children of Israel who left Egypt and never reached the Promised Land because they perished in the wilderness. I have often wondered how it is that so many people can leave a place of bondage but never reach a place of promise. Many of us end up somewhere in the middle of where we have been and where we should have gone. Perhaps we become too focused on where we left instead of where we are going. The goal is not just to go halfway. The people of old sang, "Lord, I'm running, trying to make a hundred. Ninety-nine and a half won't do." They didn't settle for mediocrity. If you realize that there are a number of possibilities that God has just for you, then you won't have to be jealous of anyone else. What God has for you, is for you. There are houses, cars, and businesses with your name on them. You should rejoice when other people get something. What disturbs me is how some people cannot rejoice with others. Instead of rejoicing they give that person pseudo-praise, but down inside, they are burning with jealousy. Real joy is when you can celebrate someone else's blessing, when you can thank God for what He has done for your brothers and sisters, knowing that what He did for them, He can do for you. God has no respect of persons. What He has done for others, He can do for you.

For every promise, there are enemies. One of the reasons Joshua and Caleb were the only Children of Israel to make it to Canaan is because of their confidence in believing they were able to take the land. I am convinced that the moment the promise goes out about you, the enemies come in.

In the book of Job, it is written, "Now there was a day when the sons of God came to present themselves before the Lord, and Satan came also among them." [1] Satan declared that he had been going throughout in the earth and walking up and down in it.[2] For every blessing with your name on it, there is an enemy on your back. If you think you are going to get your blessing without going through trouble, trials, and tribulation, you need to think again. When it is all over, God is going to give you power to not only seize your blessings, but also to defeat your adversary. God is going to give you enough strength to look at the enemy and say, *"You meant evil against me, but God meant it for good."* [3] If it were up to the enemy, you would not be as successful as you are. In spite of his attempts to destroy you, you are still blessed. As a matter of fact, if some of your friends had their way, you would not be standing on the edge of a promise, about to get what is yours. God told Moses to possess the land, but to Moses's detriment, he wanted to check it out first. He thought that it was his job to determine if the land could be taken or not. What he didn't realize is that the battle was already won. You don't have to check out what God has told you to possess. Just go possess it.

All the miracles Jesus performed should be a reason to celebrate, but it can make you disappointed in the disciples of Jesus. Considering all the time they spent with Jesus, they still didn't "get it." In the book of Luke, Jesus said to His disciples, *"Let us go over unto the other side of the lake."*[4] You can discern two things in that message: "us" should have meant for them, "Jesus, and me." Also, "other side," meant they had to survive the journey. Enemies of possibilities came in to steal the promise that Jesus made to His followers. Many people erroneously assume that on their way to the other side, his followers encountered rain or a typhoon, but the only thing they encountered was a great windstorm. They encountered the wind. The wind had a great illusionary impact, making the storm seem worse. Jesus was not worried about the wind. He was asleep in the rear of the boat on a pillow. Could it really have been that bad? If Jesus is taking you with Him to the other side, and is not worried about the journey insomuch that He could take a nap in the midst of a windstorm, you should calm down. God has already said that you are going to be all right.

Three enemies of possibilities came into their lives: fear, doubt, and ignorance. Nothing paralyzes a believer like fear. We often think that fear is natural, but it is not natural to a child of God. Stop being afraid! God needs bold soldiers. Fear is often caused by the expectation of trouble. We expect things to go wrong. If you have perfect love, it should cast out your fear.

The next enemy of possibilities is doubt. Doubt is the enemy of faith. What the disciples doubted was that Jesus cared for them. They had the audacity to say to Jesus, after he had just fed them with loaves and fish, *"Master, carest thou not that we perish?"* [5] When there is a possibility with your name on it, don't let the enemy make you doubt whether God cares for you because you don't have it yet. God cares for you, regardless if you lose your job, or even if someone walks out on you. In fact, while you are going through it all, God still cares for you. God has always loved you even in the midst of your trouble. God continues to love you. Rebuke the enemy of doubt, because the antithesis of doubt is faith. *"Now faith is the substance of things that are hoped for, the evidence of things not seen."* [6] If you can see it, it's not faith. Faith is what you can't see, but you know it's there. Faith is stepping out on nothing and knowing that before your feet hit the ground, they will touch something. Faith eliminates doubt. That is why Jesus asked the disciples where their faith was. They had no faith and were afraid because they did not know Jesus.

The third enemy of possibilities is ignorance of your creator. After Jesus calmed the wind, the disciples asked themselves a ridiculous question, *"What manner of man is this, that even the wind and the sea obey him?"* [7] This was the same Jesus who healed the woman with the issue of blood, the same Jesus who healed the leper. The question is if we really know the Jesus we sing about? If you really knew Him, you would know what Jesus could do. When you are blessed, don't act surprised. Act like you expected God to do it. If you really knew Him, then you could sleep in a windstorm. You could rebuke the wind and say, *"Peace, be still."* [8] If you've been promised, why are you worried about the wind? God has issued a word about your destiny, and yet you worry about the wind that comes out of the mouth of a naysayer. Hold on to the word and ignore the wind. It's just wind. Have you ever been sick and Jesus healed your body? Have you ever been broke and still paid your bills? Have you ever been hurt because someone walked out on you, and in the midnight hour, Jesus stepped in and made a way out of no way? Then you know Him for yourself!

When Moses gave blessings, Caleb asked for the mountain. Caleb waited for forty-five years for his blessing. You see, God will keep you and preserve you until you get your blessings. God is working on you. Don't let others put you down because of what you don't have. It's not your time yet. You may have been waiting for a breakthrough. Five years ago, it was not your time. Last year was not your time. If you get it forty-five years later, you can stand before the Lord and be as strong as you were when you first received the promise. God is about to pour you out so many blessings that you will not be able to receive them all. Regardless of how long it takes, do not forget your promise from God.

When the adversary tries to take it away, remember that it belongs to you. It's yours; a world of possibilities awaits you. The possibilities are now up to you. God has empowered you to go out and conquer that which you thought could never be conquered. It's yours. You may be going through the worst times of your life right now. God's promises may seem null and void, as if they have no effect in your life now. It is not over yet. Say no to fear. Say no to doubt. Say no to ignorance. All your life, the adversary has told you that you cannot have what God has promised. Know that what God has for you is for you!

If you are not getting the things that you thought you should have received a long time ago, you should examine whether any of these enemies of possibilities are prevalent in your life. In some instances, all three exist in a person's life. Some people are afraid, doubtful, and ignorant. No wonder you can't get what God has for you! While one of these enemies of possibilities may keep you from getting your blessing, all three of them leave you without a chance of ever getting what God has for you. These are self-inflicted enemies. Other people can't make you fear or doubt. You have to make the decision of whether you are going to exhibit any of these behaviors. That's why I like to live in the *"choose to do"* world. *The Power of Focus* by Jack Canfield, Mark Victor Hansen, and Les Hewitt identifies two types of people: those who *have to do* and those who *choose to do*. I live my life as one who chooses to do things. In everything I do, I want to be able to say, "This is my choice. I don't want others to dictate to me what I've got to do." You don't get upset because others make you upset; you get upset because you choose to get upset over what others did. It is your choice. No one can steal your happiness except you.

CHAPTER FIVE

Yes, It Can Happen to You!

Ask, and it shall be given you; seek, and ye shall find; knock, and it shall be opened unto you: For every one that asketh receiveth; and he that seeketh findeth; and to him that knocketh it shall be opened. Or what man is there of you, whom if his son ask bread, will he give him a stone? Or if he ask a fish, will he give him a serpent? If ye then, being evil, know how to give good gifts unto your children, how much more shall your Father which is in heaven give good things to them that ask him?

Matthew 7:7-11

Before encountering Jesus, the disciples never had anything. They were considered by some in that day to be rejects; then, the Savior, the Master, the Great I Am, said to them, *"Ask and it shall be given unto you, seek and ye shall find, knock and the door shall be open unto you."* [1] Jesus was about to open up a world of possibilities for them. Jesus was giving them an opportunity to liberate themselves, to liberate their minds to think from that day forward that all things are possible in their lives. You also have to live your life believing that "Yes, it can happen!" and "Yes, it can happen to me!" No more self-defeat. Haven't you beaten up on yourself long enough? Some people let the enemy go on vacation. He doesn't have to bother you. You give yourself enough self-inflicted punishment and pain. Then you want to say, "Look at what the enemy did." No, you actually did it to yourself. What comes out of your mouth and what comes out of your heart are tools of the adversary. You give the adversary an avenue to take advantage of what's going on in your life.

Too many of us are not walking in the possibilities that God has for us. We go to church and do "churchy" things, yet we are not walking in the possibilities of God. One of the reasons we don't is because we refuse to ask; we refuse to seek, and we refuse to knock or to go after what we want. James says, *"We have not because we ask not."* [2] Those are awesome, powerful words! We are not talking about superficial, repetitious words. Some of us stop at asking God, because seeking and knocking implies action. In life, some things are indeed obtained by simply asking for them. As a sophomore in college, I sold Britannica Encyclopedia's and went to a dear church mother's house to sell her a set. She fed me, gave me something to drink, gave me dessert, and we talked for over an hour. I left the house without ever having asked her to buy an encyclopedia. My sales manager at Britannica asked how it went, and I told her that I had a good meal and a good conversation, but I had forgotten to ask. My purpose for being there was not to eat her delicious meal. It was to sell her a set of encyclopedias.

That's how we are sometimes; we get sidetracked about asking God for what we want. We holler, wallow, skip, shout, and fall out, and God is waiting for us to ask. We tell everyone else our business, but we fail to get on our knees and ask God for our desires. There is a cliché in business: "No business is given to those who don't ask." Suffice it to say, I didn't last very long as a seller of encyclopedias, but I learned a valuable lesson: If you don't have the courage to look people in the eyes and ask for what you want, you will never make it in business.

When you are trying to make a deal and you make a sales call, always remember not to leave without asking for the business. Don't let others sidetrack you. This church mother knew that I was coming to sell her an encyclopedia, and she didn't want to tell me no. After she fed me, talked to me, told me how wonderful my father, Bishop Jackson, was and how proud she was of my being in college, she led me to the door, saying, "Keep up the good work." I had no sale. After that, I learned to eat their food and drink their tea, but still ask them for their business. That's what we've got to do. I don't mind asking people to be saved. I ask people, looking them in the face, to join us and be a part of God's family.

Some of you are too ashamed and afraid to ask God for what you want. You may be suffering from the fear of rejection. A good salesperson learns to accept rejection, smile, and move on to ask someone else, but if you let people who say no to you get on your nerves, you will never get anything. You should not lose one night's sleep because of what others say about you. If you are going to be successful, you've got to move on and stay focused on what God has asked you to do. Jesus told His disciples that if they abide in Him and His words abide in them, they can ask what they will, and it shall be done unto them. The problem is that we don't want to abide in Him or for His words to abide in us. We want to do the asking without the abiding. We want the promises of God, but we don't want to do what God has asked us to do, which is to remain faithful to him. God has made you a promise, and all you have to do is remain faithful and accept what God has.

Consider the Children of Israel. I blame their leadership. I believe that failures are usually the result of failed leadership. People usually follow when they are inspired and motivated and understand. True leaders find a way to get it done.

And the Lord spake unto Moses saying, Send thou men, that they may search the land of Canaan, which I give unto the children of Israel: of every tribe of their fathers shall ye send a man, every one a ruler among them.[3]

These weren't just ordinary men whom the Lord instructed Moses to send. They were rulers sent to search out what God had already given them.

And Moses sent them to spy out the land of Canaan, and said unto them, Get you up this way southward, and go up into the mountain: And see the land, what it is; and the people that dwelleth therein, whether they be strong or weak, few or many.[4]

What difference did it make if the people in the land were strong or weak or few or many? God had already said it was theirs. Moses was told to send rulers; instead, he sent spies.[5] No wonder the spies were confused. Their instructions were wrong from the beginning. Thank God for Joshua, and Caleb, and their confidence that they were able to take the land. Moses should have trusted the one who told him that it was there.

Jesus said to ask, seek, and knock. Ask God for what you want. Don't ask for just any job. Ask for the job of a lifetime. If you walk upright before the Lord, He will not withhold any good things. The only way God would deny you is if your request would be to your detriment. Give God the rights to veto any request that will cause you harm in the long run.

Jesus also says, *"Seek and you shall find."* If you have asked for something, then seeking it means that you are expecting it. If you have asked God for the job, it stands to reason that you are getting up, getting dressed, getting your résumé together, going on an interview with an expectation that you will get what God has for you. To seek means to look for it, to expect it. The question is whether you believe that you deserve a blessing. If you feel that you have been beaten down all your life, and people have told you that you are not worth anything, you begin to believe them. But the enemy is a liar! You don't even know yet what God has for you. The best is yet to come!

After you have asked and gone out to seek what God has for you, then He says, *"Knock."* Too often, we have read words in the Bible that really weren't there. All my life, I've read the scripture, "Knock and the door shall be opened." What it really says is, "Knock and *it* shall be opened unto you." He may not be talking about a door. He may be talking about a window or the roof, or He may be talking about opening the whole universe to you. It implies effort. Matthew Henry says in his commentary that asking requires faith; seeking requires action; knocking requires perseverance, the ability to stay there until you get it.

You've got to have the "stick-to-itiveness," as did Jacob with the angel who wrestled with him all night. Jacob did not turn the angel loose until the angel changed his name.[6] Jacob needed an identity transformation. The angel touched Jacob and afflicted his body, but Jacob never turned loose. You should keep knocking and be tenacious of your rights. People are going to lie about you and step on you, but keep knocking. Wounded in his thigh, lame the rest of his life, Jacob paid a price for his persistence, but he got what he asked for. Jacob's name was changed to Israel. To be blessed like Jacob, you can't give up. Be persistent.

CHAPTER SIX

Yes, We Can

But I rejoiced in the Lord greatly, that now at the last your care of me hath flourished again; wherein ye were also careful, but ye lacked opportunity. Not that I speak in respect of want: for I have learned, in whatsoever state I am, therewith to be content. I know both how to be abased, and I know how to abound: every where and in all things I am instructed both to be full and to be hungry, both to abound and to suffer need. I can do all things through Christ which strengtheneth me.

Philippians 4:10-13

We looked earlier at the enemy of doubt, fear, and ignorance. The enemy of doubt is something the enemy brings your way to try to steal your promise and your possibilities. *Doubt can be defined as the lack of confidence in what has been promised.* That lack of confidence is the enemy of your possibilities, which comes into your mind and prevents you from having faith in what has already been promised. The Bible is a book of promises, from Genesis to Revelation. These promises are given to those of us who walk upright before the Lord.

It is the desire of the adversary to come in to steal, kill, and destroy your possibilities. He tries to get you to doubt what is already yours. It is what has been promised to you; it is your promise from God. It does not make sense to doubt if the promises of God are yours. He has confirmed that they are yours. Adam and Eve's whole existence was of God, yet Eve let the enemy influence her to doubt God's word. Read any chapter in the Bible and in it you will find a promise of God. Doubt hinders us from getting those promises.

Doubt is like a roadblock. A roadblock doesn't mean that there is no road on the other side of the block. It simply means that something is standing in the way of where you need to be. Doubt comes in when you choose to stay on one side of the roadblock. You choose to stay because the enemy is the master of deception. His whole game is smoke and mirrors. He cannot deal with substance because he does not deal in truth, so he plays a mind game. He played one with Eve and tried to do so with Jesus in the wilderness. He tried to convince Jesus to turn stone into bread, knowing that Jesus was hungry after having fasted for forty days. Your adversary knows how to bring what you need at the worst times in your life. You have to be strong enough to say to him, as Jesus said, "Get thee behind me." [1] You've got to rebuke the enemy. Jesus responded with a word from God. You've got to respond to the enemy with a higher authority, an authority that he understands, not with a feeling, a belief, a wish, and a hope. You've got to respond, *"It is written…."* You've got to know that God says that you are blessed going in and coming out. The word is the authority. The enemy knows that if he can get between your promise and its manifestation, he can stop you in your tracks, and you will die without ever receiving your promise. You will die broke, even though there was a rich inheritance that was laid up for you. You will die hungry, even though there was food on the other side of the roadblock. You will die lonely, although peace and joy were on the other side of the pain you had to go through. When doubt creeps in, you are no longer listening to God. You are now listening to the adversary. You are stopped in your tracks.

Since the opposite of doubt is faith, don't get upset when you can't see your possibilities coming to fruition. It's a faith opportunity. There are times in your life when you can't see how you are going to make ends meet. It's a faith opportunity. You may be going through a difficult situation right now. It's a faith opportunity. You've got to stand up and say, *"It's a faith opportunity."*

I refuse to let the enemy plant seeds of discouragement in my mind. Les Hewitt, in *The Power of Focus,* says that everything you want in life is on the other side of your doubt and your fear.[2] It is not about whether other people doubt your abilities. That does not matter. What matters is if you doubt your abilities. If Ben Carson had listened to the counselors in the schools of Philadelphia, he would have never become one of the greatest neurosurgeons in the world. They told him he was "slow" and had a learning disability, which would require him to attend special schools. What they did not know was that something special was going on inside of him. When God empowers you, God can make all the critics wrong. Have others given up on you and said that you can't make it? What matters is if you believe it.

We need to infuse our young people with a dose of confidence that they can do anything they want to do. What we are missing today in our selfish society are people who are willing to be mentors, who will take young people, shape them, and mold them. I remember vividly, people such as Henry Ponder and Benjamin Elijah Mayes from Benedict College, who would teach young men like me. When segregation ended and integration was forced upon us, we had to go to certain places, where we knew that stereotypes had automatically branded us. The enemy had separated us by race, but God was bringing people together, black and white, brown, and yellow.

There are young people in your lives right now who have been told what they cannot do, and they are giving up, as opposed to doing more. Encourage them not to give up. If they have a hard time learning how to read, you should find the time to help them. You should turn the television off. We are glued to the television that feeds our entertainment side and not our intellectual side. Quite often, the reason we lose hope and possibilities is because we lose focus.

Faith is hope in the unseen. Your faith opens up possibilities in your life like no one else's faith can. In other words, people can't pray blessings upon you; some blessings your faith must open up. You may have been told that you cannot achieve, succeed, or prosper. Enough negativity will make you begin to doubt what God has said. Doubt begins to skew your perception of what you hear and what you see. When you allow doubt into your mind, it begins to destroy your life. You begin to read more into everything. You begin peeping out windows and checking cell phones, and if you are not careful, doubt will destroy your relationships. You cannot live where there is no trust.

Likewise, you will not succeed spiritually if you will not trust God. You need to know that God will bring you out of a bad situation. You cannot question God's loyalty to you. You nearly lost your relationship with God because you lost faith and trust in Him. Rebuke the adversary. Don't give up on God. Don't get an attitude with God. You may have to go through some challenges, but in the name of Jesus, yes, you can! You are more than conquerors. Paul says, *"I know how to live on almost nothing or with everything. I have learned the secret of living in every situation, whether it is with a full stomach or empty, plenty or little."* [3]

Your mindset should not change if you catch the bus or drive a Mercedes. Can you live in prosperity? If you get the job, go to sleep with joy. If you do not get the job, still go to sleep with joy. Learn to be content. Learn to trust in Jesus. Whatever state you are in, be content. Bless the Lord at all times. Let His praises continually be in your mouth. Regardless of what you are going through, you should still love God. Every day is a good day. From this day forward, strike from your vocabulary the phrase "a bad day." There are no bad days. If you are above ground, it's a good day. Is it well with your soul?

CHAPTER SEVEN

No More Fear

...I will fear no evil...

Psalm 23:4

For God hath not given us the spirit of fear; but of power, and of love, and of a sound mind.

2 Timothy 1:7

Perfect love casts out all fear. It is impossible for perfected love to exist where fear exists. There will be either love or fear. They cannot coexist. You have to choose which one will reign in your life. We can be conquerors of our fear. Fear is a deadly enemy to the world of possibilities. If there is anything that will stop your possibilities, it is fear. It will prevent you from being where you need to be, from having what you should have had a long time ago. It is a debilitating emotion that will paralyze the human spirit. It restricts your mobility. It hinders you from doing things you should do and from going places that you should go – simply because you are afraid to stand up and face your fear. It amazes me how people who are so holy can be so afraid. Jesus chastised His disciples when He said, *"Why are ye fearful, O ye of little faith?"* [1] Jesus had a problem with those who hung around Him for three and-a-half years and were still afraid of a little windstorm. In order to conquer fear, you need to do more than memorize scriptures; you need to apply them and believe what you speak. Fear wants to prevent you from applying the scriptures and believing. Fear is designed to stop you from getting what God has for you.

Fear is a strong negative emotion caused by the anticipation of danger. Fear is not the danger itself, but the expectation of danger. You expect bad things to happen. It doesn't make any sense to walk around expecting bad things to happen in your life. It doesn't make any sense to invite the adversary to come into your life just because your mindset isn't strong enough to refuse to allow something that you don't know for sure will happen to dominate your mind. However, let me be clear: You will have trouble. Job says, *"Man that is born of a woman is of a few days and full of trouble."* [2] That should not to be a surprise to you. What you should know, however, is that for every trouble in your life, deliverance has already been prepared. You need to know that.

Fear strikes when you don't think that you can come out of what you are in. Fear strikes when you think that life will not get any better. Fear strikes when you sit there and say, "I am going to die of this." Faith, on the other hand, is saying, "If I die, there is a building of God, a house not made with hands, eternal in the heavens." [3] You have to face fear and not allow the adversary to control your position by something that does not yet exist. That is what God wants us to understand. What should separate us, as believers, from others is that we walk by faith. It isn't that we have more than the world has, but we have faith. We have the ability to look at nothing, and believe that something will be there. Why? It is because our faith is not in what we see, but in what God has said about us.

Fear isn't just being afraid. It is debilitating. Look at what fear does to your natural body. It accelerates your heartbeat. It puts you in an emotional frenzy in which you become extremely hyper and agitated. Many psychologists believe that there is a side to our nature that enjoys some degree of fear. That is why movies like *Nightmare on Elm Street, The Exorcist,* and *Halloween I, II,* and *III* are watched by so many. People enjoy the jolt that comes from the roller coaster called fear. I don't watch horror movies. If the adversary is going to make me afraid, I refuse to help him do it. Joy, peace, and euphoria come in the absence of fear. Fear keeps you on the edge, and if you keep experiencing it, you will want it over and over again. After fear occurs, your heart rate drops as though you were on a roller coaster.

I don't understand why people choose to ride roller coasters. Afterward, they are trembling, having thrown up all over you. Their money has dropped to the ground, and yet, they are excited and want to ride again. Some people enjoy things that are not always healthy for them. They have been living on the edge for so long that they don't know how to live without fear. They've been living in fear for so long that they continue to push the limits, not knowing the sense of peace and tranquility that God has given them in the absence of fear. They have substituted peace with the anticipation of danger. Zig Ziglar says that fear stands for false evidence appearing real.[4] You cannot enjoy the life that God has given you because you are worried about something that doesn't exist. If you walk around encouraged, you tell the adversary that you refuse to let fear dominate your life. If you know that something exists, you should not fear it because perfect love casts out all fear. I am not saying that you will not be afraid.

It is not practical, neither is it wise, prudent, or good guidance, to say that you will not experience fear, because you will. There will be times in our lives when we will all face fear. So, the question is not if we will face fear. Rather, what will we do when we are face-to-face with fear? You will be confronted with fear in your daily walk. You are going to have to deal with situations that are going to make you nervous, put you on edge. You will get bad news that will change your mindset. The challenge then becomes what you will do next. The phrase "fear not" appears 365 times in the Bible. Why do you think that God spent so much time putting this one phrase in the scriptures, "fear not; and be not afraid"? If heaven and earth will pass away before one tittle or jot fails, what about something that is in the Bible 365 times?

When I was a student of law, we had study groups using a Socratic method of studying. We only had one exam at the end of the semester. People would often go crazy from the stress. Some of those students who were in my study group are doing very well today, while others are not. The ones who were very fearful failed. It wasn't that they were not smart. I remember a young woman in my first year at USC School of Law who was brilliant, and she had a great educational background that would cause you to think that she would be very successful; but she was very afraid. She was much smarter than me. She was usually nervous in the study group. In those classes, law professors intentionally tried to intimidate you. Our professors had us stand up in a class of more than 100 students, and drilled us. This young woman could not handle that sort of pressure. I remember a particular professor who had her stand before the class and he drilled her so badly, she broke down in tears. At the end of the semester when the class grades were posted and she learned how poorly she had scored, she had to be placed in an institution. She had the ability to do much better than we did, but she could not do what she was gifted to do because she lacked the confidence she needed, and fear had set in.

Law school requires a tremendous amount of reading and writing. This young woman was an exceptional writer; she told me that she had been reading on a ninth-grade level when she was in the sixth grade. Yet, a professor in one day changed the course of her life. She lacked the ability to face obstacles and say, "come at me again. I missed that question, but come at me again." What is the purpose of this illustration? To let you know that the enemy is playing a Socratic method on you. You already have the ability to do whatever you want to do, but he has stolen your heart. In other words, he stole your confidence. He has told you that you don't have the courage to face your adversary. You don't have the courage to say, "Yes I can."

Others have told you that you can't do it, that you will never be anything; that you are going to be a failure just like your father, and all the while, the adversary is stealing your heart. You know that you have what God has given you to make it, yet you don't have the courage to stand up and say, "Yes I can." What difference does it make if you fail once if you succeed in the end? Every great person who has ever done anything has failed at some point in his or her career. History records their successes, because they had the perseverance to stand up every time. Franklin Delano Roosevelt was once asked what made him successful. His wife Eleanor Roosevelt responded that he got up one time more than he was knocked down. What a powerful word! In the end, they recorded him as the author of great federal bills like social security and veterans' benefits. This was a man with polio, who was told to give up. He had something on the inside of him that made him keep going. Do you have the right stuff inside of you, such that every time you get knocked down, you get back up? So what if you got fired – you are not the only one who has ever gotten fired! You are not the only person to be laid off of a job, but you have to have the right stuff inside of you so that when you get knocked down, you get right back up. You see, it is not what's on the outside of you. It is not what you have on; it is not what devastating news you are hit with, but it is what is inside of you that makes you get up again. Your enemy is trying to steal what you have inside of you! He wants to place doubt and fear inside of you so that when you are knocked down, you stay down. You've got to get back up again! Have the strength and courage to get up. God has not given you a spirit of fear, but of power and of love and of a sound mind.[5]

> *And they brought up an evil report of the land which they had searched unto the children of Israel, saying, The land, through which we have gone to search it, is a land that eateth up the inhabitants thereof; and all the people that we saw in it are men of a great stature. And there we saw the giants, the sons of Anak, which come of the giants: and we were in our own sight as grasshoppers, and so we were in their sight.[6]*

It is one thing to miss out on something you never had, but when it is yours, when it has been promised and delivered to you, and you cannot get it because of your fear, that is disappointing. The men Moses sent to spy out the land of Canaan agreed that the land was plenteous; they agreed that it flowed with milk and honey, but they felt that they could not take the land. That was the problem - they did not have to take the land. God told them to possess it. If they had gone there and simply sat on the land, God would have driven the enemies away. How can I prove this statement? Consider the city of Jericho before they stepped foot on the other side of the wall. God had already prepared for the enemies to be driven out - walls fell down; the enemy had to leave. Moses's group did not have enough faith or enough courage because of perceptions and the anticipation of danger. When they looked at the outward appearance of their adversary, their response was to declare that the men of Anak are giants. They come from giants. They are huge.

Because the Children of Israel thought of themselves as grasshoppers, so were they in the minds of their enemies. They did not conquer the battle raging in their minds. The greatest warfare you will ever encounter will be what goes on between your ears and your brain. It will determine what you think about your situation and what you think you can or cannot do. There are so many people with a defeatist attitude. They feel as if they cannot do it. Ask successful entrepreneurs, if given a choice when hiring, what traits they would like, and they will undoubtedly choose a person with a can-do attitude. You have to be willing to lose everything. You have to be willing to face things that you are not sure about and say, "Yes, I can."

The difference between the Children of Israel and King David is that David was younger. David did not have the experience they had, yet he had enough experience to trust God. When David was faced with fear, he did three things:

1. He recognized what fear was: a spirit. Fear is a spirit that transcends boundaries and will go where you go. King David had to recognize that he was dealing with a spirit. David wrote, *"Create in me a clean heart, O God; and renew a right spirit within me. Cast me not away from thy presence; and take not thy holy spirit from me."* [7] He knew that his problem wasn't with Bathsheba or that he had more testosterone than anyone else did.

2. King David confronted his fears. When David's brothers were hiding in a ditch, he could have done what his brothers did, but he didn't. They were hiding from a giant called Goliath. Giants are just those things that are bigger than anything else. You've got giants in your life that you must face. When David's brothers asked him what he was doing at the battle, David replied, *"Is there not a cause?"* [8] In other words, there is a reason that David was standing there. *"David said moreover, The Lord that delivered me out of the paw of the lion, and out of the paw of the bear, he will deliver me out of the hand of this Philistine. And Saul said unto David, Go, and the LORD be with thee."* [9] You have to have faith to believe that God can do it! He has done it before. If he did it then, he can do it now. You have to get rid of fear and cast it on God. When David knocked Goliath down, he didn't go to celebrate, because the job was not finished. You shouldn't be

content by knocking your giant out. You must destroy evil. Having knocked Goliath out, David took Goliath's sword and cut his head off. He did this because he knew that a knocked-out giant could get up again! Don't just knock down your fears so that you can sleep one night. Take care of your fears so that you can sleep the rest of your life! Take action that will give you the courage to do what you need to do. If you are going to conquer fear, you've got to finish the job.

3. Rely on God's word. God's word will give you the strength to do what you have to do. Don't be afraid anymore. Go face-to-face with your fear. Just as David did not run from Goliath, he did not run from Absalom. The names of your enemies may change, but the circumstances are still the same. David never ran from any of the Philistines. David had God on his side. Have the courage to face fear head-on and say, "No more fear!"

CHAPTER EIGHT

To Know Him

"That I may know him, and the power of his resurrection, and the fellowship of his sufferings, being made conformable unto his death;"

Philippians 3:10

"...for I know whom I have believed"

2 Timothy 1:12(b)

Do you know Jesus? Do you know Him enough to give you a comfort level of trust? Truly knowing Jesus means that you know that He will not allow you to go through anything that would ultimately destroy you. Apostle Paul tells us, *"There hath no temptation taken you but such as is common to man."* [1] In all the things we go through, God will give us a way to escape. I know that about God. I know going into a situation that it is not going to be more than I can bear. There are enemies of possibilities that come into our lives to steal, to kill, and to destroy the possibilities that God has for us. In essence, God has already established a promise concerning your life, yet there are areas that can impact your access to these possibilities: doubt, fear, and anxiety. If you are a person who is prone to worry, your health could be at risk. You can eat right and exercise, but if you are a "worry-wart," the chances are that you will die sooner than those who do not. It's called stress. A lot of stress is self-induced. Because we are stressed, we worry over what doesn't even exist.

Neither does God want you to be nonchalant about life. While God wants you to trust Him, it does not take the place of your responsibility to do everything that is necessary. Not wanting to work, being slothful, lazy, and overly content is a spirit that stops you from receiving the possibilities of God. God is not going to allow you to have everything dropped in your lap. Some things you've just got to get out and do. We should not allow the enemies to come in and be a substitute for the things that we can control in our lives. Fear and doubt are deadly lethal enemies that will sidetrack you from what God has for you in your life, yet there is another enemy, ignorance, which is what you do not know. A common expression is that *"a fool is someone who doesn't know and doesn't know that he doesn't know."* In some areas in life, we can't know everything, but we've got to strive to know the things that are important to our spiritual development; that is to know God. What you don't know *can* hurt you.

Have you ever had a relationship with someone whom you did not give yourself time to really get to know? You rushed into the relationship, and it went from a casual conversation to having lunch now and then, to talking on the phone at night, and the next thing you know, he has moved in. After he moved in, what you didn't realize is that he is not as clean as he looks. He has no job, no money, and he treats you like dirt. Then you declare that you did not know. Well, whose fault is that? You did not take time to get to know him. You rushed into that relationship, and as a result, you had to pay the price. I would rather you take the time and be by yourself a little longer than to rush into things. There are some crazy people out there these days, both men and women, who may not let you walk out of a relationship. The funeral director will have to roll one of you out of that house! You need to know people before you get involved with them.

Take your time and get to know people, because knowledge is powerful, and usually, people will not stray from their history of behavior. Leopards have a hard time changing their spots. In other words, if he abuses her, you can believe that he is going to abuse you. If he didn't pay the light bill when he was married to her, chances are he won't pay it for you. If she didn't cook then, she won't cook now. You've got to learn that people don't typically change.

That's why I like methodical thinkers, those who take their time. Sometimes they can aggravate you because they are so deliberate and patient, but usually, they make fewer mistakes because they think the situation out, they look at all sides; then, they make a decision based on knowledge.

There are things about God that we should know. By studying Him, looking at what He has said, and looking at what He has done, we get to know Him. God says through the Prophet Hosea, *"My people are destroyed..."* [2] God chose to use this strong word. They are *destroyed*. He did not say knocked down; He did not say sidestepped; He did not say delayed. He also said, *"My people."* Christian believers are destroyed for a lack of knowledge. The verse continues, *"...because they have rejected knowledge."* [3] This indicates that knowledge is something that you must choose to embrace. They did not want to know.

There are some who are proud of their ignorance. There are some who don't want to know anything. They just want to come to church and shout and not know anything about God's word. If you know God, and you know His word and the history of the Bible, you know that trouble comes into good people's lives. You understand that there were tumultuous situations in the lives of people who loved God. But you also know that God brought them out all right.

You need to know the God whom you serve. Ministers can't just throw anything out to someone who is serious about his or her faith. Don't shout "amen" and fall down over just anyone preaching, regardless of whether it is right or wrong. I once went to a service where I heard a preacher speak for five minutes in all kinds of languages. People were falling out - they had no earthly idea of what he was saying. I asked the Lord what the people were rejoicing about. Another time, when I heard someone in the pulpit speaking in tongues for several minutes in the middle of his sermon, I thought to myself that I came to this service to hear someone to speak to my heart; I wanted him to say something that I would understand. Before I can get excited about something, you've got to speak a word of understanding to me. I don't fall out and get excited about just anything, I've got to hear you and understand what you are saying. If you just want to rejoice over the fact that God is good, we can do that! All of us can do that. We can have a corporate praise and a shout, but when it comes down to God's Word, speak to me.

My father loved to say, *"Speak to my mind."* He used to tell us as ministers in the church, to speak to people's minds, speak to their hearts, and give them something they can hold on to. You've got to be willing to speak so that others can hear and understand. *"In all thy getting, get understanding."* Invest in a good Bible. Do your shoes cost more than your Bible? Do your fingernails cost more than the Bible they hold? Why can't you invest in a study Bible that introduces the chapter before you read it, that gives you the footnotes, and tells you who wrote it and the year they wrote it and what the application of scripture is? Why can't you invest in that? Is it because it is not a passion for you? Your passion proceeds out of your heart. If you have a passion for God's Word, you will study God's Word and not treat Him in any haphazard way. You would take serious your worship of God and your service to Him.

Too many of us are spiritually lazy. We say our nightly prayers thirty seconds before we go to sleep. What kind of relationship is that? If you were in a marriage or a dating relationship and only spoke to each other for thirty seconds' worth of conversation a day, you would not be together long, because that relationship could not last. How do you think a relationship with God is going to last if we do not communicate with Him and get to know Him? The greatest way to get to know God is to ask Him to speak to your heart, and He will give you an individualized prophetic word just for you — not just a corporate word. You'll never get it if you don't have quiet time with God. It is what the Bible is referring to when it says, *"Be still and know that I am God."* [4] Turn the radio off, turn the CD off, and get your word from God. Ask God to speak to you and watch God speak to you and give you unspeakable joy. Get to know your God.

God rejected Israel because Israel had rejected knowledge. God was angry with them because they did not take the time to get to know Him. An acquaintance and awareness of something is not knowledge. The word "know" is an intimate word used in the book of Genesis when it talks about consummating a relationship. Adam knew Eve. We know what the Bible means, because later came Cain and Abel. When you know someone, it is an intimate relationship. It is when you fit together with that person and you become one. That's how you get to know your God. *"They that know their God shall be strong and do exploits."* [5] The

Bible says that you can do wonderful things when you get to know your God.

I know that I have a covenant relationship with God, and He has promised to open the windows of heaven and to pour me out a blessing. This tells me that God has a benefit plan. Know what you are entitled to in God. What God has done for others, He can do for you. Your benefit plan is based on your having an intimate relationship with God. The difference is not some academic, logical relationship with God. There are a whole lot of people who can quote scriptures but can't live right. Don't be impressed with people who can "talk-the-talk." Make sure they can "walk-the-walk." The adversary quoted the scriptures to Jesus in the wilderness. He took the scriptures out of context. Jesus knew the spirit of the scriptures. It's more than being able to memorize a verse; it's being able to live by the principles and the concepts of that verse. Do you love your neighbor as yourself? It is worthless if you know every book of the Bible, but you can't speak to your neighbor.

Don't be too impressed with the outward things, but watch God work on the heart. God will make you love your enemy and treat everyone nicely. The actions of the disciples, as written in the book of Mark, have stuck with me. While they were on the boat, not only did they *not* know God, but also they didn't listen to what He said. He told them that they were going to the other side. They weren't paying attention. His words never penetrated their hearts. It never became an intimate situation with them. So when they got into trouble, they had forgotten what they should have known. They woke Jesus, accusing Him of not caring about them. Jesus became angry because of their faithlessness.[6] They should have known that this Man has the power to speak to the wind and the rain and say, *"Peace, be still."* [7]

But when the struggle came, they ran and hid because they did not know Christ. You are getting ready to go through storms in your life. Rocky situations in your life are about to surface. Do not get upset, and do not threaten mutiny because things are not going your way. Get up in the midst of your storm and say, "I know in whom I believe." What a powerful word! And if God brought you to this situation, God is certainly able to bring you through it. The reason the disciples could not have faith is because they all had a surface relationship with Jesus. They ate His fish, His bread, took His money, and allowed Him to pay their taxes. They enjoyed the status of being near Him while 5,000 people were drawing near, but they really did not know Him. When Jesus was hanging on the Cross, with the exception of John, His disciples were not there. John was the only one who was there with the women. Even so, something happened on the day of Pentecost, because what was around them was now in them. On the day of Pentecost, their relationship was consummated. When Christ dealt on the inside of them, Christ's power gave them the strength to stand in the streets of Jerusalem and speak to the men and women who cheered the crucifixion of Jesus. The difference was that the knowledge of Him was now internal, not external. Get to know Jesus on the inside. A song cannot do that for you. You must put His word in you and invite His spirit in you. The Holy Spirit comes by invitation only. It is freely given, but you must invite it in. Others can't pray the Holy Spirit over you. You've got to get somewhere by yourself and ask God to fill you with His anointing spirit. If you do so, the things you used to do and the places you used to go will change. God will change the desires of your heart.

It wasn't until I really got to know Jesus that I no longer cared what my friends thought, because my desire to please God had changed. If Jesus defeated the enemy, so can you. If Jesus can look down from the Cross in the faces of men who had just pierced His side, put nails in His hands, and asked the Father to forgive them, how much more can *you*? God is giving you the keys of the kingdom so that whatsoever you bind on earth will be bound in heaven. Use the keys. Let it go. Turn it loose.

CHAPTER NINE

Anger: An Enemy of Possibilities

Ye have heard that it was said by them of old time, Thou shalt not kill; and whosoever shall kill shall be in danger of the judgment: But I say unto you, That whosoever is angry with his brother without a cause shall be in danger of the judgment: and whosoever shall say to his brother, Raca, shall be in danger of the council: but whosoever shall say, Thou fool, shall be in danger of hell fire.

Matthew 5:21-22b

Be ye angry, and sin not: let not the sun go down upon your wrath: Neither give place to the devil.

Ephesians 4:26-27

In the Gospel that was recorded by Matthew, Jesus spoke what is known as the Sermon on the Mount. Many scholars agree that this is one of the most profound spoken words in all biblical history. More than any other, it reflects who Jesus is, as well as His mission, and His purpose.

How we deal with anger is one of the most challenging and complex issues we will ever face as believers. What is amazing to note is the number of Christians who have trouble controlling their anger. There are people who are angry with

73

God. Your anger will dictate how you worship. If you do not properly handle anger, it can be a dangerous, destructive emotion that will ultimately bring you down. Anger can be harmful, dictating your physical, spiritual, and emotional well-being. You become emotionally out of control when you cannot take your anger and make it subordinate to your will. Because you are angry with someone, you may miss the reward of God. You must remember that anger will separate you from what God has for you.

It is not the big things; it is the little foxes that spoil the vine. It is not as severe as your attempting to steal or wanting to shoot someone; it is people getting on your last nerve. You can't control other people, but you can control yourself. Uncontrollable anger is one of the leading factors in domestic violence cases. There are husbands and wives of the Christian faith who have not spoken for the past month. They have pent-up hostilities against each other, and yet they come to church to serve as deacons and ushers and worshippers. Before you serve anyone, you should fall on your knees and say, *"It's me, oh Lord, standing in the need of prayer."* Studies have shown up to 40 percent of children who commit violence have witnessed some form of violence in their homes.[1] A lot of children are imitators of their parents; they become what they see! For instance, how can you expect them not to go to school and fight if you are fighting and cursing each other in your home? I believe the reason they are violent is because they see violence. They see you lose your temper. You want to excuse it as a character flaw. If you have been born again, you should act differently. If you love the Lord the way you say you love Him, people should not get you that upset. Anger is responsible for splitting up families and businesses, and yes, even splitting up churches. You've got Christians fussing and fighting, angry at one another.

In Genesis, Cain, the son of Adam and Eve, and the brother of Abel, lost his cool and killed his brother because of hostility, jealousy, and anger.[2] Those of you who cannot control your tempers are easy targets of your enemy. Don't make it so easy for the enemy. He doesn't need any help. You have to be able to praise God on good days and on bad days. It is not the person with whom you are angry who suffers. You suffer more than he or she does. It is *your* hair that starts falling out. It is *your* blood pressure that goes up. The perpetrator of the deed against you is living life to its fullest, while you are walking around upset with your blood pressure high, and you can't sleep at night. Get over it! Let it go! People could care less if you are upset. Most people don't even know that you are upset with them, and those who do are proud that they could get you upset. It takes more than a gossiping tongue, and feet that bring bad news, to steal my joy! You have to learn to have joy in the middle of tribulation.

In all of the bad anger discussed in this chapter, there is something called good anger. It is called indignation. This anger comes about when you are upset with the "wrongs of life" but not to the point that it is detrimental to your health. If you are angry that people are starving in Africa, that's righteous indignation. If you are angry that this government is spending more money on bombs than on healthcare, that's righteous indignation; however, it should not be to the point that you hate the president and cannot sleep at night and it adversely affects your health. Jesus says, *"Whosoever is angry with his brother without a cause is in danger of the judgment."* [3] The verse before that says, *"Ye have heard that it was said by them of old time, Thou shalt not kill; and whosoever shall kill shall be in danger of the judgment."* [4] Unjustifiable anger is equated with murder. It is just as bad as killing someone, because you are going to be in danger of the same judgment. In other words, you are going to burst hell wide open because you are walking around angry at things that should have been settled long ago.

Jesus is teaching us that we have a responsibility as believers to control the emotions that would separate us from our possibilities. Get over it! You are not the only one who has been hurt. People have been hurt since the beginning of time. Get over it. It's been too long. You have been holding on too long. Deal with it. There is a cause for righteous indignation, and we should at times expect to get angry, but it should not control us to the point where we sin. It is one thing to be upset. It's another thing, however, to curse someone out. There should be a difference in our lives as believers. If you have the Holy Ghost, you have been baptized in the Spirit of God, and you walk with God, you should not let things get you angry. There are three things that you can do to help you control your anger and keep it from controlling your possibilities: **Reflect, Restrain, and Release**. Reflect on your actions. Take a breath and think about your actions before you act. Have discipline over your emotions. Do not react instantly. You should have enough wisdom in you to reflect before you react. When you think about it, ask God if it is in His will. Don't instantly react.

Exhibit godly restraint before you react. The only way for you to have godly restraint is to have the Holy Spirit. You need to choose your words carefully. Holy Ghost restraint will make you smile when people have just cursed you. Take these words out of your vocabulary: *"I've got to get this off my chest."* Think about what it costs you. The worst thing you can do is let others know that they have gotten to you. When the enemy says "yes," the Holy Ghost will say "no." David wrote, *"For I said in my haste, I am cut off from before thine eyes: nevertheless thou heardest the voice of my supplications when I cried unto thee."* [5] Every time he said something "in haste," it was to his detriment.

Thirdly, you've got to turn it lose. Release it. Take your burden to the Lord and leave it there. Don't go to bed with pent-up anger. The word "release" simply means to set free. Let your past pass. You should march on to something greater. Turn anger loose. Let it go. It's not worth it. People will always have something to say. Don't allow the enemy to come in and steal your promise because you are angry with people on your job, in your home, even at God. Apostle Peter wrote, *"Casting your care upon Him; for he careth for you."* [6]

Chapter Ten

Limited Thinking: An Enemy of Possibilities

And Caleb stilled the people before Moses, and said, Let us go up at once, and possess it; for we are well able to overcome it. But the men that went up with him said, We be not able to go up against the people; for they are stronger than we. And they brought up an evil report of the land which they had searched unto the children of Israel, saying, The land, through which we have gone to search it, is a land that eateth up the inhabitants thereof; and all the people that we saw in it are men of a great stature. And there we saw the giants, the sons of Anak, which come of the giants: and we were in our own sight as grasshoppers, and so we were in their sight.

Numbers 13:30-33

For as he thinketh in his heart, so is he: Eat and drink, saith he to thee; but his heart is not with thee.

Proverbs 23:7

Of all the other ones, fear, doubt, anger, ignorance, etc., limited thinking controls how you handle the rest of your life. It is important that you conquer limited thinking, which is small-time thinking; having a defeatist attitude; thinking as if you don't deserve to be where you are.

The enemy is the master of deception. He is all smoke and mirrors. His strategy is to have you think that he is more powerful than he is, but all he can ever do to you is influence you. Consider the book of Genesis and the Gospels in the New Testament, in which the adversary directly approaches others; He approaches Adam and Eve in Genesis, and Jesus in the wilderness. In neither situation could he make them do anything. Adam and Eve sinned because the adversary convinced them to do it. If he could have made them do it, he would have saved himself a whole lot of talking. Instead, he worked in their minds. The adversary didn't have the power to zap Adam and Eve and say, "Pick up that fruit and eat it." He did have the ability, however, to influence their will, to influence their thinking. Ultimately, the decision to sin was theirs. I always look at people strangely whenever they say, "The devil made me do it." No, he convinced you to do it yourself, but he did not literally pick your hand up and make you slap somebody. He can't literally go in your mouth and utter curse words out of your mouth to someone else. He can go into your mind and convince you that this is what you want to do, and you then make the decision to do it. The enemy does not have that type of power. He isn't as powerful as we give him the credit to be. People have made the adversary out to be this supernatural hero. You act as if the enemy can just walk up behind you and make you do something, make you jump in somebody else's bed, make you break up somebody else's home. It doesn't work like that. We blame it on everybody. We are big on this generational curse excuse, which allows you to blame your bad behavior on everyone else. In essence, what you are saying is that it is your mother and father's fault.

Where the adversary succeeded in convincing Adam and Eve, he failed in convincing Jesus. Jesus did not allow the adversary to get into his head the way that he gets into some people's heads. He has defined for us who we are going to be. In your mind, He has shaped your future. Have you already declared failure before you even begin because the enemy is in your head?

It is tactical not to let him get in your head. Some business people that are negotiating and closing deals play mind games. You may say in negotiations, "Take it, or leave it," and you are packing your bags, getting ready to leave, but you are hoping that they will take it. They are thinking about whether to call your bluff. It is a mind game until someone blinks, until somebody says, "I give up; I need what you are offering." The enemy has gotten into your head and told you some things that hinder you. God told you that you could. The enemy told you that you couldn't. Whose report will you believe? It is called limited thinking. Caleb and Joshua were confident that they were able to overcome the giants in the land of Canaan. The other ten spies were concerned about themselves.

You see, when you pay more attention to individuals than to the challenge, you lose. Too often, we fail in conquering the challenge because we have a "them" mentality. It is not about the circumstances which God has given you the strength to overcome; it's about who said it. We get so bent out of shape over people, who they are, what they think of us — the "them" mentality. Caleb and Joshua saw the same thing. Caleb knew that they were able to overcome it. *"But the men that went up with him said, We be not able to go up against the people; for they are stronger than we."* [1] Who said anything about the people? They concluded that because of what they saw. They had never known anything about the sons of Anak. Appearances can be deceiving. They had already given them value, based on what they saw, not on what they knew. *"They are stronger than we are,"* the spies said. How did they know? Did the sons of Anak walk across the Red Sea on dry land? Were they delivered out of Egypt under the mighty hands of God? Did they eat manna from heaven? Did they drink water from a rock? The other spies said they could not overcome *"the people,"* but Caleb said they were able to overcome *"it."* What was Caleb talking about? The "it" was that circumstance that stood in the way of his promise. Caleb didn't even give it the respect of naming "it." Are you so focused on who it is that has done you wrong that you fail to realize what it is that has done you wrong? *"We wrestle not against flesh and blood..."* [2] It is not about "them"; it's about "it." It is about you conquering that thing that has held you down. No longer will it discourage you.

Why does the glass have to always be half-empty? Why do we focus on the negative? We can see one teenager who messes up, and we want to talk about the youth and how misguided they are. What about all the wonderful teenagers who do well, who go to school and study, come to church, and are no trouble at all? It is because we've seen the negative. Our opinion has been shaped by our perception, and we usually see what we want to see. In the book of Numbers, you will find one of the most powerful verses in scripture, which says, *"And there we saw the giants, the sons of Anak, which come of the giants: and we were in our own sight as grasshoppers, and so we were in their sight."* [3] Isn't that powerful? Because they said that they were nobody and nothing, they were looked upon as nobody and nothing. When you say you are a loser, other people will call you a loser. You have already formed your own opinion about who you are. I refuse to allow anyone to define me as long as I am a child of God.

John C. Maxwell says in his book, *Thinking for a Change,* which successful people think differently than unsuccessful people.[4] Successful people will see a glass half-full. Unsuccessful people will see the glass half-empty. It's a mindset. It's a matter of how you think. Our actions are interpreters of our thoughts. We do what we think. There are no actions done without thinking. Perhaps you did not think a situation through thoroughly, but you gave it some thought; therefore, you triggered an action. Maxwell says if you want to change your life, change the way you think. In order to get a different crop, you must plant a different seed. If you want happiness, plant seeds of joy. If you want peace, plant seeds of peace. You cannot hang around people who cause confusion and think that you will sleep peacefully at night. You've been around chaos all day long. If you want to sleep well, think well.

Finally, brethren, whatsoever things are true, whatsoever things are honest, whatsoever things are just, whatsoever things are pure, whatsoever things are lovely, whatsoever things are of good report; if there be any virtue, and if there be any praise, think on these things.[5]

Here is the challenge: If we are able to curse limited thinking, defeat limited thinking, change our mindsets, we can achieve greatness. People who achieve greatness believe they can do it. Don't allow the enemy of limited thinking a place in your life. *Now faith is the substance of things hoped for, the evidence of things not seen.*[6] Hope is not for the things you already have in your possession. Hope is for those things you want to have. *But without faith it is impossible to please him: for he that cometh to God must believe that he is, and that he is a rewarder of them that diligently seek him.*[7] Even before you get your rewards, you've got to believe that God can give you a reward. Sure, you can shout over what you have, but can you shout over what you expect to have? Can you give a praise of expectation? Before you come to Jesus, you've got to know that He can do it. Before you call Him, you've got to know that He can answer. Before you get sick, you've got to know that He is a healer. Before you get confused, you've got to know that He is a mind regulator. Change the way you think. Think defeat no longer, but victory. Think poverty no longer, but prosperity.

How do you see your giants? There are some giant challenges hanging around you. There will be challenges that you will have to go through. A pink slip is a challenge. A negative doctor's report is a challenge. You have no money in your bank account and the bills are due, that's a challenge. You get tired of going home every night by yourself, that's a challenge. There are three questions you have to ask yourself:

1. What do I think of myself? It doesn't matter what other people think of you. What do you think of yourself? Apostle Paul says, *"I can do all things through Christ which strengtheneth me."* [8] Do you qualify for that scripture? Whenever the enemy tells you that you cannot have it, tell him it's too late.

2. What do I think of my situation? Apostle Paul says, *"And we know that all things work together for good to them that love God, to them who are the called according to his purpose."* [9] It is one thing to have a positive attitude about yourself,

but do you believe whatever you are going through has to work out? What do you think about the trials and tribulations that you are going through? What you are going through has to work out for good because it fits under the scriptural term, "all things," including cancer, strokes, and high blood pressure. Sometimes you don't know why you are going through what you are going through, but you know that God is going to work it out. You have to be qualified. It won't just happen if you are not qualified. It happens to those who love God, to those who are the called. We have been trying to figure out *our* purpose, and we need to know *His* purpose.

3. What do I think of my God? He never would have brought you to it if He could not bring you through it. You know that no weapon formed against you shall prosper. You know that the earth is the Lord's and the fullness thereof. You know that His seed shall never beg bread. *But my God shall supply all your need according to his riches in glory by Christ Jesus.*[10]

If you know who you are, if you know about your situation, and if you know about your God, you have just broken the chains of limited thinking. There is no situation that you will encounter that is not common to man.

CHAPTER ELEVEN

Pride: An Enemy of Possibilities

All this came upon the king Nebuchadnezzar. At the end of twelve months he walked in the palace of the kingdom of Babylon. The king spake, and said, Is not this great Babylon, that I have built for the house of the kingdom by the might of my power, and for the honour of my majesty? While the word [was] in the king's mouth, there fell a voice from heaven, [saying], O king Nebuchadnezzar, to thee it is spoken; The kingdom is departed from thee. And they shall drive thee from men, and thy dwelling [shall be] with the beasts of the field: they shall make thee to eat grass as oxen, and seven times shall pass over thee, until thou know that the most High ruleth in the kingdom of men, and giveth it to whomsoever he will....

Daniel 4:28-37

Pride [goeth] before destruction, and an haughty spirit before a fall.

Proverbs 16:18

Pride is an enemy of your possibilities. The Lord hates seven things. The first one He lists is pride.[1] It even comes before a lying tongue. It is truly an enemy of your possibilities, and we must deal with these enemies that come from within.

86

They are not imposed on you. They are not placed on you. They are not forced on you. If you really want to get to know a person, get to know his or her thought process. See how he or she acts under pressure. People can conceal their true feelings when the sun is out, but when the storms come, they say, "Master, you don't care if we perish." When the storms come, the truth comes out of people. Real personalities emerge out of struggles.

How do you react when you are angry, upset, abused, or overlooked? All of us can develop bad attitudes when we think we have been overlooked. We have to deal with our attitudes and bring ourselves into submission. It's not about you. It's about who you are. If you aren't careful, pride can destroy you. *"Pride goes before destruction and a haughty spirit before a fall."* [2] Apostle Paul says, *"For if a man think himself to be something, when he is nothing, he deceiveth himself."* [3] Stop deceiving yourself. You think that others have bought into your game when most have already noticed who you really are. You just didn't realize that they knew. Some people act as though they are important, thinking that they are "the greatest things since sliced bread." No one can do it as he or she can. Shakespeare said in *Hamlet,* "To thine own self be true..." [4] We've got to be true to ourselves and stop deceiving ourselves. I always say, "Lord, help me to not be a distraction to *me.*"

Sometimes others will give you extravagant praise, and you start believing them. God, however, wants us to stay humble. In order to do that, you've got to keep your feet firmly on the ground because the people on your job may tell you that you are the best employee and that they can't do without you. But, if you are terminated, your colleagues will smile in your face, telling you goodbye, when it's time for you to leave. Guess what? They will get back to work the next morning. Life goes on.

I will admit that when I was young and mischievous, I used to make fun of church people. I would attend funerals with my friends and watch those family members who were grieving to see how long it took them to go eat chicken and pound cake at the repast. The dirt had just been thrown over their loved one, and they had just affirmed that they could not live without the recently deceased; yet they would come back from the burial ready to eat and socialize. Perhaps they *are* grieving on the inside, but they are in the process of getting over their loss. As sad as we all may be, we go home and go back to work in a few days. In other words, people get over you. As much as people love you, they get over you when you are gone. People will mourn you, and if you are widely known, they may even put a monument up for you. But eventually, they will continue on with life. That's why we should not think of ourselves more highly than we are.

People are resilient and bounce back. You allow God to heal your hurt. Solomon says, *"Let another man praise thee, and not thine own mouth; a stranger, and not thine own lips."* [5] If you have to promote yourself, there is something wrong. As a pastor, I often preach that you need to encourage yourself. There is a difference between encouraging yourself and bragging about yourself. If the only recognition you get is when you've got to do it, there is something wrong. The greatest marketing tool in the world is not a thirty-second ad; it's not a magazine article; it's a satisfied customer. The greatest restaurant ads come when others tell you that the food is good and you take their word as a witness. Your life should be such that others say something good about you. You don't have to promote yourself. You don't have to praise yourself. Do something so that others can see your good works and glorify your Father, which is in heaven. Solomon also said, *"He that is of a proud heart stirreth up strife: but he that putteth his trust in the Lord shall be made fat. He that trusteth in his own heart is a fool: but whoso walketh wisely, he shall be delivered."* [6] Don't trust in your own ability. Trust in the Lord. We have to learn how to trust in God and not depend on ourselves.

There are different types of pride. The good type is justifiable self-respect. There is a reason you should respect yourself. The bad type is when you are self-centered, self-righteous, and arrogant. In other words, when you are just full of yourself! If the truth were told, we have all been there at some time in our lives. It's human nature to go through that. That's why we have to know how to submit ourselves under the mighty hand of God. We must say, "Lord, help me work on me, that I won't take things at face value; and not think of myself more highly than I should, because if I do, it is an enemy of my possibilities."

In general, people do not like to be around those who are always touting their own accomplishments. You can't get three words out of your mouth before someone is reminding you of who they are, who they know, and what they do. People will find a way to avoid a bragger. For this type of person, when they fall, people will celebrate their demise, whether warranted or not. They will do it simply because of how the bragger treated others in his or her lifetime. Be good to others because you may need them to be good to you. Be kind to others because you may need them to be kind to you. Smile at others because you may need a smile one day. Give others the benefit of the doubt. One day you may need someone to give you the benefit of the doubt. Be careful that you don't become arrogant when you are on top.

When my cousins and I were young, my grandfather gave us corn to feed the chickens. Instead of feeding the chickens, we would throw the corn at them to watch them run. That wasn't what he had in mind when he gave us the corn. So he taught us how to take that same corn and feed it to chickens delicately so that they would eat it from our hands. That lesson reminded me of how some Christians take the good news of the gospel and treat it like corn in their hands. If you have thrown it at them and scattered them, you can't expect them to consume it.

We often run people away because of our own ego and pride. I believe one of the greatest hindrances to Christianity is other Christians. They see our hypocrisy and say, "If that's the way it is, I do not want any part of it." If that's the way they treat their brothers and sisters, by throwing the gospel at them because they made mistakes along the way, I do not want any part of it. But when you walk humbly before the Lord, the reason you can't treat people like that is because you remember where you have come from. You remember where God brought you from and how God delivered you. You were not as spiritual as you are now. You struggled with things. But God gave you a second chance.

Why is it that the people who have been forgiven the most are the least forgiving? As senior pastor of the Bible Way Church of Atlas Road, I don't concern myself with what people say about our letting anyone in the church. I am proud that anyone can come to our church. In fact, you can be a prostitute on Saturday and come to our church on Sunday. Why? Because this is not our house. It is God's house. You don't turn away the sick from the hospital. Nor should you turn away a sinner from the church. You have been delivered too many times to act stuck up. We have come through a lot and it was God who delivered us. God loves all of us, regardless of what we all are going through.

King Nebuchadnezzar had a problem. He thought it was all about him until God brought him down. He kept saying, "Look at my kingdom; look at my majesty; look at all that I have done with my own hands; look at how great I am." God drove him from the kingdom. He made him crawl on the ground like a wild animal. He knocked him on his backside in order to get his attention.

King Nebuchadnezzar learned three things from his experiences:

1. He learned to praise, exalt, and honor the Lord and not to praise himself. His losing everything taught him that. It was not about him but about God. He learned to extol and to praise the Lord God Almighty.

2. He learned that the works of the Lord are true and His ways are just. He learned that God is in charge. Your ways are not God's ways. Don't try to find your purpose for your life. Seek, instead, to find God's purpose for your life. Remember this about God's punishment: His judgment is just. It is just what you deserve. In the book of Malachi, God says that He will open the windows of heaven and pour out blessings. God will give you options. You see, pouring is a consistent flow. You may have had a drizzle for so long until you think that your drizzle is a pour. You haven't seen anything yet. God is getting ready to pour out your blessings. When you call your friends, let them know that it is pouring in your life. Get ready for the options and the choices. Get ready for more than enough.

3. God can bring you down if you are too high. I have made a conscious decision that I will humble myself. I do not want the Lord to humble me. I will do it myself.

CHAPTER TWELVE

The Spirit of Religion: An Enemy of Possibilities

And as he spake, a certain Pharisee besought him to dine with him: and he went in, and sat down to meat. And when the Pharisee saw it, he marvelled that he had not first washed before dinner. And the Lord said unto him, Now do ye Pharisees make clean the outside of the cup and the platter; but your inward part is full of ravening and wickedness. Ye fools, did not he that made that which is without make that which is within also? But rather give alms of such things as ye have; and, behold, all things are clean unto you. But woe unto you, Pharisees! for ye tithe mint and rue and all manner of herbs, and pass over judgment and the love of God: these ought ye to have done, and not to leave the other undone. Woe unto you, Pharisees! for ye love the uppermost seats in the synagogues, and greetings in the markets. Woe unto you, scribes and Pharisees, hypocrites! for ye are as graves which appear not, and the men that walk over [them] are not aware of them.

Luke 11:37-44

Having a form of godliness, but denying the power thereof: from such turn away.

2 Timothy 3:5

The spirit of religion is one of, if not *the* most, deadly enemies of possibilities. The spirit of religion is those traditions that you put in place of godliness and righteousness. In fact, this enemy separates you from your spiritual destiny. Because it is too easily disguised, the spirit of religion is deadly. It is readily overlooked by those of us who are "called to be saints."

There are more wars that have been fought over religion than anything else. One of our spiritual songs of old, *Onward Christian Soldier,* was written by those who thought that they were doing the work of the Lord by taking on the enemy through force. The spirit of religion has hurt more people than pride, greed, anger, doubt, fear, ignorance, and limited thinking all put together.

God said to the nation of Israel, *"I hate, I despise your feast days, and I will not smell in your solemn assemblies."* [1] He also said, *"Take thou away from me the noise of thy songs; for I will not hear the melody of thy viols."* [2] In other words, He could not tolerate their worship experience because they were hypocritical. The Amos passage did not refer to religion per se, but to the spirit of religion, an enemy of possibilities. God does not despise people; He loves people. He wants someone who is not trying to get limelight attention. Amos was written in 760 B.C. Years later, Paul wrote *"Traitors, heady, high-minded, lovers of pleasures, more than lovers of God; Having a form of godliness but denying the power thereof."* [3] A spirit of religion will separate you from where God wants you to be.

Some of us are too religious for our own good. We have taken what was supposed to be holy fellowship, and we've made it into a social club, fraternity, sorority type of atmosphere. You like this person; she is in. You don't like the other person; she is out. This one is accepted, the other not, and God despises that. If we are going to be a light unto the world, others should see our good works and these works should glorify our Father who is in heaven. When men and women see you, they should see Jesus in you. Some of us are a distraction to Jesus. When people see us, they don't want to know Jesus because if Jesus looks like some of us, others would rather not meet Him. Be careful. You are better off not knowing God than knowing God and becoming an albatross around someone's neck. You may cause someone to miss the Kingdom. You go to work and claim to be one way, and then afterward, you are cursing, fussing, lying, and stealing. Your spirit of religion is the enemy of your possibilities.

What is the spirit of religion? The great noted theologian C. Peter Wagner, a professor of theology at Fuller Theological Seminary, defines the spirit of religion as "an agent of Satan assigned to prevent change and to maintain the status quo by using religious devices." [4] The spirit of religion is the belief that you will be saved by your works, that your deeds can substitute for your heart, and the things you do in church or in religious settings are all that is necessary so that you can go to glory. The spirit of religion says that because you have been baptized, you are saved; because you are a leader in the church, you are all right. That is not the case. Your deeds cannot save you. If you have walked in darkness all your life, it is now time for you to come to the light. Baptism doesn't save you! Deeds can not save you.

Your religious deeds are just an example of religious change. Baptism is submergence in water to signify that change has occurred. If your heart hasn't changed, you go down a dry sinner and come up a wet sinner.

There is a spirit that allows people to think that because they are in a religious experience, they have all that they need and they don't need anything else. Dr. Wagner goes on to say that the spirit of religion promotes the idea that what you do is more important than who you are. In other words, you think it is more important that you go to church, sing in the choir, and pay your tithe every now and then.

This spirit of religion thrives on rituals, traditions, and ceremonial events. It judges you by the clothes you wear, the size of your Bible, and how many passages you can quote from memory - all of the things that you *think* make you holy. So you know where to find Habakkuk in the Bible. You know the creed of the church and are a stickler for the traditions and the history of the church, but can you walk upright? Thank God for the men and the women who may not know how to quote scriptures, but will say, "For God I live and for God I will die, and to God be the glory."

Religion has created denominations, but denominations are not found in the Bible. Denominations are a product of our egos, to have a reason to separate. Denominations allow some to claim to be Pentecostal and others Methodist. Some are Baptist and others are Southern Baptists; there are Presbyterians and Episcopalians. People will change churches if it is not the right denomination. Your focus should not be your denomination, but your determination! It means that you should stand on faith, love, peace, and joy and treat people like you want to be treated.

The spirit of religion takes the place of faith. It takes the place of your walk with God. There are some people who are so obsessed with the institution of religion that they forget the walk of faith. They can tell you when you misquote a scripture. They can tell you when something is not in ecclesiastical order. We have been hoodwinked. Jesus told the woman at the well that they that worship Him must worship in spirit and in truth. He came to change the order of things so that Jews and Samaritans could sit down together.

One of the greatest examples of the spirit of religion is when Jesus accepted an invitation from a Pharisee to come to his house to eat.[5] They thought that they were setting Jesus up, but Jesus was setting them up. This Pharisee considered himself to be an ordinary lay leader who came up by his own bootstraps. Pharisees were literal in their translation of the law. Their religion became their Achilles' heel. When they invited Jesus, they noticed that Jesus violated one of the premier ceremonial rituals of the day with the ceremonial washing of hands. It was required that you wash and purify your hands. This was their tradition. They had a certain way that they washed their hands to indicate that they have been purified from the lack of cleanliness of the world. When Jesus came in, He sat down to eat. They could not believe that Jesus had violated their tradition. Jesus admonished them by calling them fools for being more concerned with the outside than the inside. They should have asked God to wash them from the inside out.

Young people seem to think that older people are traditionalists; however, some of the most progressive members of my church are the older members. I shall never forget the late Mother Josephine Anderson. She will always be dear to me. Whenever we wanted to take a new direction in the church, Mother Anderson was supportive of our initiatives even when she didn't understand or agree. Those who have been around for a long time do more than talk this gospel. They walk it. This means that you walk by faith. You have to trust things that you don't understand but know that if God said to do it, then it is the right thing to do.

Those who gave Jesus the hardest time were the religious leaders. They were protecting their turf. You see, the spirit of religion was not indicative of the masses of the people. The masses of people were following Jesus. They did not know enough about scriptures to make theological decisions. Religious leaders did not want them to know about scriptures. Jesus was revolutionary. He chose to associate Himself with and bring into His inner circle, women, lepers, and tax collectors. Jesus did not care about traditions. He came to do a new thing.

Being against the spirit of religion does not mean that you are for the spirit of secularism or the spirit of hedonism. It does not mean that you subscribe to the theory that you should eat, drink, and be merry, for tomorrow you die. There has to be a healthy balance. The Lord is looking for someone who is neither super-religious nor carnal. The Lord is looking for people with spiritual balance in their lives. Some people are still offended by what you wear on the outside, instead of how you are feeling on the inside. They don't understand that ministry is more important than protocol. Some people would come into the church, sit there, and miss an anointing because their spirit is grieved about how you are dressed. The only one who wins that victory is the enemy. In the times that we are living in, we must be able to strike a healthy balance. This does not mean that you should dress inappropriately. The Holy Spirit should convict you. I refuse to be anyone's moral police. My calling is to convince you that you need the Comforter that will lead and guide you into all truth. When people see you, they should see Jesus. Would Jesus mind being you?

The Pharisees in the Bible were separated people. They were a little less educated than the Sadducees. They believed that they earned their position and deserved respect. They could not get beyond ritual ceremony. You had to address them in their ecclesiastical titles. Their good intentions were used for evil results. The enemy does the same thing today. How do others outside church see you? It is fine to have a sense of order, but it cannot go to your head. The Pharisees were separated and strongly monotheistic. They believed in one God and accepted the Old Testament's authoritative Word of God. They affirmed that angels existed, and that demons existed, and they believed in life beyond the grave. They were missionaries seeking to convert other gentiles. They were strong in what they were trying to do, but their lives became obsessed with rituals.

The Sadducees were aristocratic. They had more money than the Pharisees did. Their bloodlines were from a rich, priestly line of order. They would fight over who got the biggest recognition. The Sadducees stood in opposition to the Pharisees. To the Pharisees' credit, they were a strict group of religious Jews who advocated obedience to the minutest portions of the Jewish law and traditions. The Sadducees, however, wanted money, fine linen, and other material things.

The Scribes were the professional interpreters of the law, who especially emphasized the traditions. Zealots, on the other hand, were the extreme wing of the Pharisees. They believed that only God had the right to rule over the Jews. They were willing to fight and die for that belief.

There was one thing that brought all of these opposing groups together - they were all opposed to the ministry of Jesus

Christ. Jesus was a threat to each one of these groups. When you read your Bible and see that the Pharisees, Scribes, Sadducees, all came together, that is amazing all by itself. They all despised Jesus because Jesus was a threat to them; He was a threat not to their faith but to their spirit of religion.

CHAPTER THIRTEEN

Blessings and Curses: A World of Possibilities

Behold, I set before you this day a blessing and a curse; A blessing, if ye obey the commandments of the LORD your God, which I command you this day: And a curse, if ye will not obey the commandments of the LORD your God, but turn aside out of the way which I command you this day, to go after other gods, which ye have not known.

Deuteronomy 11:26-28

In your world of possibilities, you have choices to make and you must make those choices yourself. Choices are not easy things to make because of the consequences. When you choose a direction, things happen as a result of your choosing to go one way or the other. The thing that is important for us to note is that God does not make the tough choices for us. He did not do it for Adam, and He will not do it for you. That is why God, who gave Noah enough anointing to build the ark, also gave him the leeway to get drunk before he left the ark. Noah had enough anointing to build the ark for 120 days, yet I imagine God saying to him, "It's up to you. You have to decide whether or not you are going to come out." Noah chose the pathway that led to his demise. As a result, corruption happened on the face of the earth that was inhabited by Noah and his family.

God does not make up your mind for you. He does not choose which door you walk through. He is not going to do that. He has set before you an open door. You must choose to go through it. God said, *"Behold, I set before thee an open door..."* [1] — walk in and get your blessing. It takes no will of your own for people to push you through an open door. On the other hand, it does take something for you to stand at the crossroads in your life and ask yourself the question, *Am I going to choose the way of blessings, or will I choose the way that leads to curses?* God will ultimately hold us accountable for the choices we make. Blessings occur when the hand of God is on you. In the Old Testament, the blessing was equivalent to those in authority laying hands on you. Some Christians buy prayer rags and anointed oils so that others will bless them. They think it's a magical potion that they can buy. Not so. For young adults everywhere, there are choices, and for not-so-young adults, there are choices.

Oftentimes when we face the unpleasant consequences of our choices, we want to blame others for where we are. That's when we give the enemy too much credit. If the adversary were that big and bad, he would have destroyed you a long time ago. He is not as smart as you think he is. We must be able to live with the results of the choices we make. If you want to be set free, you have got to change. It may have been years since you have done what God has asked you to do. Do you have to go backward to make it right? The answer is *no*. I believe in the forgiveness of God.

However, I do believe that if you feel led to go back and make it right, God will accept your sacrifice. Just as Jesus said to the woman who was caught in the very act of adultery, when He looked at her and said, "Go and sin no more." [2] Note what He *didn't* say. He didn't say, "go find the person who you did this to and get it right." He meant, from this day forward, go, and sin no more. If you want to be delivered just say, "Lord, I'm sorry. I ask for your forgiveness. And from this day forward, I will walk in the newness of life." If you believe that, today is the first day of the rest of your life!

Too many of us are obsessed about what we did not do yesterday. God is concerned about what we are doing today and about what we are going to do tomorrow. The past is gone. Let it go. You've got to embrace where you are and plan for where you are going. God will forgive you for the errors of the past. God will deliver you. He will welcome you into His kingdom. Just because you have fallen short doesn't mean it's over. God can give you a brand new start and tell you go and sin no more. You have to choose to be delivered. God has set before you an open door, which will either allow you to be blessed or allow you to be cursed. There is no chapter in the Bible that gets my attention like Deuteronomy 28. If you want to be shocked into reality, read that chapter. Verses one through 14 deal with the blessings of God; verses 15 through 68 deal with the curses of

God. Every time I read them, I am in awe of what God said can happen. Clearly, God does not want to pronounce curses upon you. Rather, God says that when you choose the path of destruction, these are things that will happen to you. If you want to walk in the fullness of joy, you must choose the path that you are going to take.

When you do not obey God, these curses will come upon you:

1. **The curse of the land.** *The Lord shall make the pestilence cleave unto thee, until he has consumed thee from off the land; whither thou goest to possess it.*[3] God is going to send pestilence to take your land of promise if you do not obey Him. The Israelites had no land in the wilderness. They could not even change the shoes on their feet. When God takes His hands from you, the pestilence will come upon you and devour the land that you have. You may own the land, but you can't enjoy it. While you own the land, the enemy owns the atmosphere. The atmosphere is not conducive to your enjoyment. You are in the place that you should be, but you don't have the protection of God. The curse of the land is a situation in which the enemy comes and takes what is promised to you, you won't be able to enjoy it. You may have gotten a new house, but you cannot enjoy it because you are not obedient to

God's Word. You can barely pay your mortgage. You can't keep one light on in two rooms at the same time because you cannot make ends meet. Every time the phone rings, you think someone is coming to take your possessions. You are in the place that you should be in, but you cannot enjoy it because God has sent pestilence to eat up your land.

2. **The curse of the enemy.** *The LORD shall cause thee to be smitten before thine enemies: thou shalt go out one way against them, and flee seven ways before them: and shalt be removed into all the kingdoms of the earth.*[4] *The LORD shall bring a nation against thee from far, from the end of the earth, as swift as the eagle flieth; a nation whose tongue thou shalt not understand; A nation of fierce countenance, which shall not regard the person of the old, nor shew favour to the young.*[5] Not only is the Lord not going to allow you to enjoy your land, but also your enemy is going to come and take your land. You will see someone in bad shape if you look at someone who used to know the Lord and doesn't know Him anymore, someone who has lost everything he had. You will notice that those who were saved and left the faith look worse than those who have never been in the faith. The hand of the Lord have been removed from them. When the curse of the enemy is upon you, you will have enemies that you know nothing about. God will allow your enemies to come in. What happens to you when God turns away?

I remember hearing a powerful sermon as a young boy about the Spirit leaving the tabernacle. When the Spirit left, there was corruption and destruction and abuse, and promiscuity. God says that His Spirit will not dwell with us always. Do not make a mistake about it; God will not always dwell in your mess. There may be a point in which God says, "I turn you loose." In the Book of Romans, they called it reprobate.[6] God has released you. You think you know more than He does, and you don't need any help. You don't think you need God, so He releases you. He turns you over to the lusts of your own spirit. You have sinned with all of your might until your wrong begins to look like right. You need the hand of the Lord on you.

3. **The curse of the spirit**. The curse of the spirit is a situation in which the Lord allows the enemy to come in, break your spirit, steal your gladness and your joy, and leave you with a countenance of depression. Many saints are taking medication because their spirits have been broken. They are sitting there depressed. They feel as if no one loves them. Perhaps they should examine the choices they made. If they have invited the enemy in, they have to live with the remnants of the enemy after he leaves. *"Because now servedst not the Lord thy God with joyfulness and was gladness of heart for the abundance of all things therefore shall thou serve thine enemy which the Lord*

107

shall send or allow against thee in hunger and in thirst and in nakedness and in want of all things and he shall put a yoke of iron upon your neck until they have destroyed you." [7] In other words, God says the third curse is the curse of the spirit, where you are yoked until you are destroyed or until you say, *"Here I am, Lord. I am coming out from under this. I want to give you my life. I don't care what my friends say. This is bigger than my friends."* Some of you have an anointing on you that your friends don't have. If that is you, there will be no peace until you walk in your divine purpose. You will die a hurt and broken person having never fulfilled your goals unless you say, "Here I am, Lord."

We have reviewed the curses of God. Now let us explore the blessings of God: the blessing of provision, the blessing of prosperity, the blessing of promotion, and the blessing of protection.

1. **Provision is having enough.** God has given you all that you need in order to make it. The Lord declared that He shall command the blessing upon you and your storehouse and in all that you set your hand to do. He will bless you in the land - God will give you enough in your storehouse so that you will be able to make ends meet. You will be able to make it. You will be able to go on with the help of the Lord. That's enough to praise God all by itself. But there is something else. God says

because you are blessed, He is going to give you more than provision.

2. **God is going to give you prosperity**. He is going to make you so blessed that people are going to gossip about you. He is going to make you so blessed that the enemy is going to be upset. You are about to get on the enemy's nerves and rumors will start about you. The Lord will allow you to prosper. The Lord will open unto you His good treasure. Don't desire the treasures of others; instead, desire the treasures of God. God will allow the heavens to bring rain to your land in its season and to bless all the works of your hand so that you will be a lender and not a borrower. You will have enough for yourself and others. You will be living under the blessings of prosperity.

3. **The blessings of promotion**. The Lord will make you the head and not the tail. You are about to move from the back to the front of the line. The Lord is getting ready to promote you. And you will be blessed with increase.

4. **The blessing of protection.** The Psalmist says, *"Keep me as the apple of the eye. Hide me under the shadow of thy wings."* [8] God will protect you; God will protect your family and what you have set out to do. If you are the apple of God's eye, when the enemy comes to eat up your flesh, he will not succeed. That is the blessing of

protection. In other words, even if the enemy wants to, he can't get to you because you are under the shadow of God's wings. In the time of trouble, God will hide you. In the midst of your trouble, the Lord will protect you. No weapon formed against you shall harm you. You will be under the protection of God.

Chapter Fourteen

Your Failures Have Not Ruined Your Possibilities

And he arose, and came to his father. But when he was yet a great way off, his father saw him, and had compassion, and ran, and fell on his neck, and kissed him. And the son said unto him, Father, I have sinned against heaven, and in thy sight, and am no more worthy to be called thy son. But the father said to his servants, Bring forth the best robe, and put it on him; and put a ring on his hand, and shoes on his feet: And bring hither the fatted calf, and kill it; and let us eat, and be merry: For this my son was dead, and is alive again; he was lost, and is found. And they began to be merry.

Luke 15:20-24

When Jesus had lifted up himself, and saw none but the woman, he said unto her, Woman, where are those thine accusers? hath no man condemned thee? She said, No man, Lord. And Jesus said unto her, Neither do I condemn thee: go, and sin no more.

John 8:10, 11

The enemy will try to convince you to believe that your failures have ruined your possibilities. It is the intent of the enemy to convince you and me to give up just because we've made mistakes. The enemy wants you to feel hopeless and believe that your life has been ruined. He wants you to feel as if there is no hope for you because of what you have done. If God would mark iniquity, who would stand? There is no one who deserves to be saved because of the lack of sin in his life. God's Word tells us that we all have sinned, and all of our righteousness is as filthy rags. The enemy wants you to feel that your life is ruined. The word "ruined" means "to be damaged beyond repair; complete and total destruction; collapse." [1]

The enemy tells you every day that there is no hope. He tells you that you cannot get back on your feet because of something you did. Some Christians don't make this any better. We often become willing accomplices with the adversary. The enemy brings it, and we rub it in. We become agents of the adversary. We have people thinking that their lives are over just because of a mistake that was made in their past. What we must remember is that the sense of being ruined is a mindset. That is why it is so dangerous. Oftentimes, how we think is more important than what we do. King Solomon understood this when he wrote,, *"as one thinketh in his heart, so is he."* [2]

I refuse to help my enemy out. If you are going to think badly about me, you'd better do it on your own, because I refuse to think negatively regarding who I am. Yes, I am somebody. Yes, I am special. I am all of that and more. I am not perfect. I am not immune from tribulations and trials. I have made mistakes before and will likely make mistakes again in my life. But, I'm *still* special because I am a child of God.

If you think that you are no good, think that you will never achieve, that's your mindset. In fact, that's what the enemy wants you to think. This is why the enemy tries so hard to control your way of looking at things. He couldn't care less about your body, your wardrobe, where you live, and where you hang out. He cares about how you think.

Some of you don't believe people can be saved. Some Christians sit in church and shout every Sunday but have a limited expectation concerning the salvation plan of God. The enemy has come in to control their minds. Apostle Paul says *"Let this mind be in you that was also in Christ Jesus."* [3] He also tells us in the book of Romans to be transformed by the renewing of your mind.[4]

Change the way you think. If you don't change where you are, and what you are doing, at least change the way you think. If you change the way you think, you will change what you do. Your thinking dictates your actions. Don't let the enemy take your mind. The enemy is only trying to mislead and deceive you. There are too many people walking around feeling that their lives are ruined because they have fallen short and missed the mark.

Perhaps the greatest threat to God's church is the church. We have too many sanctimonious people in church that don't even attempt to reach out to the unsaved. If the truth were told, those who have long been saved have sinned just as much, if not more, than those who are trying to get saved. You may not have experienced some of the things in which today's youth are faced with, but you have fallen short of God's glory as well.

If God saved you, why do you think He can't save our young warriors who are turning to Him? God can do it. He is transforming the church from being a place of judgment to an open door. What we discover in life is that our failures often make us better. Author John Maxwell wrote a book called *Failing Forward,* in which he said that his failures had led to his successes.[5] You may be too religious to admit that, but if you had not fallen, who knows where you would be? You had to fail at some point in your life in order to get you to where you are now. God lets us go through failures so that we can appreciate divine blessings when we get them. If you had not been through hell in your life, you would not enjoy where you are and where you are going.

There are two distinct examples of the grace of God. Grace is the unmerited favor of God; a loving God bestowing to us divine mercy. Grace includes both forgiveness and restoration. Grace is not just saying, "I forgive you." It is also restoring the relationship with the person who violated you. Restoration means taking something back to its original state. You are not totally saved if you cannot totally forgive.

If you are harboring ill feelings against someone, God is not ready to take you to the next level. Grace is forgetting, forgiving, and restoring. God forgot some things about us, having cast them into the sea of forgetfulness. He forgave us for our sins. He restored unto us the years that the locusts, the cankerworms, and the caterpillars did eat. This is God's amazing grace, grace that looks beyond our faults to see our needs. The adversary will make you feel that God won't save you because of what you have done in your past. That was then. This is now. If you come to God, you will be covered under His blood of redemption. God will forgive you for all your iniquities.

There are two examples of grace - one involving a young man who made a mistake in judgment and thought his life was ruined. The other example is of a young woman caught in a moral failure. No doubt, she did it. She was caught in the very act of adultery. She also thought that her life was over because of what she had done.

The young man was very different from the young woman, because he was of royal descent. He lived a privileged life, but he did not have a sense of inner peace. Money could not make him happy. This young man believed that he could make it on his own. He didn't feel that he needed anyone. He wanted to be his own man and to do his own thing. He left a place of provision in order to pursue a place of dreams. He left what he had, looking for what he thought was in a far away country.

This young man's dream turned into a nightmare. He lost everything he had. He had no friends, no family, no money, and no one to look out for him. He became a citizen of another country, and was put in the pigpen to feed the swine. He hit "rock bottom." He left everything he had and ended up feeding swine.

You know that you have hit rock bottom when you have to eat slop from a pigpen. Some of you may think that you don't need anyone. You don't need the Lord; you don't need the church; you don't need others to pray for you. What you don't know is that the only thing that kept you from hitting rock bottom a long time ago is that someone was praying for you. Some of you had praying mothers, fathers, grandparents, aunts, and uncles.

You had relatives living in certain regions of the country that you never wanted to visit. You may have had family members who could not put a subject and a verb together, who didn't know how to write an essay and who could not add or subtract as well as you do. You thought that they didn't have anything to offer you. What you didn't know is that while you were pursuing your dreams, someone was on his or her knees, praying for the Lord to bless you and protect you. Even though you thought you were doing everything yourself, God withheld the adversary. Just because you made a mistake, your failures have not ruined your possibilities.

My father often told me about leaving home at the age of sixteen. His mother walked down to the train station just to see him off. His father would not come. The last time he saw his mother was when she turned around to go back home. Some years later, he came home and asked his brothers and father where his mother was, and they told him that she had died. He said that he thought he was going to lose his mind upon learning of his mother's death, but God took the broken heart of someone who had been through many trials and took those experiences to use him to minister to thousands. His failures did not ruin his possibilities. He became the bishop of one of the largest churches in South Carolina.

The enemy wanted this prodigal son to think that his life was over. When he came to himself, he decided to go home. The father was looking for him. The father met him halfway down the road - the road of recovery. Before the son could say he was sorry, his father said, "This is my son."

This young man's father called a feast. He made a public declaration about the restoration of his son. The father put shoes on his son's feet. He was no longer a servant. He put a robe on his back. He was restoring his royalty. He put a ring on his finger, giving him back his authority.

Your Father sits up high and looks down low. After all you have been through, the Father still calls you His child. Other people have written you off, but God still calls you His child.

The woman's example is very different. She was an ordinary woman without any of the amenities of royalty. She was out there by herself. She was considered a "nobody," without a rich father or any hired servants. She was an underprivileged woman "looking for love in all the wrong places." She made a mistake because she trusted people. That's how it often happens. Before a woman knows it, her telephone number is being passed around. The whole group is abusing her. She thought that at least one of them would love her. The woman Jesus saved was a good person, but she was looking for someone to love her.

When she got caught, the men didn't turn their buddies in. They turned her in. What happened to the man? They brought this woman to Jesus, trembling, shaking, rejected, and dejected. She had no father to return to. There was no one to put a robe on her back. She was bowed down, and broken . Her accusers were all around her with stones in their hands. They were ready to take her life. She must have thought that her failures had ruined her possibilities. She had been caught in the very act of adultery. They had the evidence to prove it. Jesus looked at the accusers and asked those of them without sin to cast the first stone. Before the men could perpetrate a lie, He began to write on the ground.

I'd like to believe that He was writing the names of the women *they* had all been with. All of them left, leaving Jesus with the woman, still bowed down waiting to be stoned. Jesus asked her where her accusers had gone. When she looked up, she saw that they were gone. Jesus instructed her to go and sin no more. It was a second chance for her. Her failures had not ruined her possibilities.

Some of us have been wrapped around the pews too long and are no longer sensitive to other people's troubles. The young man was given a pair of shoes, a robe, and a ring: restoration. The woman at the feet of Jesus was given a word: restoration. By law, she deserved to die, but she was given another chance. Your failures have not ruined your possibilities because God is a God of second chances.

Chapter Fifteen

Will You Believe What You Cannot See?

But Thomas, one of the twelve, called Didymus, was not with them when Jesus came. The other disciples therefore said unto him, We have seen the Lord. But he said unto them, Except I shall see in his hands the print of the nails, and put my finger into the print of the nails, and thrust my hand into his side, I will not believe. And after eight days again his disciples were within, and Thomas with them: then came Jesus, the doors being shut, and stood in the midst, and said, Peace be unto you. Then saith he to Thomas, Reach hither thy finger, and behold my hands; and reach hither thy hand, and thrust it into my side: and be not faithless, but believing. And Thomas answered and said unto him, My Lord and my God. Jesus saith unto him, Thomas, because thou hast seen me, thou hast believed: blessed are they that have not seen, and yet have believed.

John 20:24-29

It is very easy to believe what you have seen. It is easy to follow the evidence. It is easy to be an expert when you are backed up with proof of what you claim. But can you believe when you cannot see it? Are you at a point in your life where you don't see a way out? If you have the faith to look on the other side of the door and believe what you have not seen, God will bless you.

Throughout the Gospels, Jesus performed many miracles. After He healed or delivered individuals, Jesus often turned to the people who had been delivered to say that their faith had made them whole. It is not just a touch or a word that goes into the atmosphere, but it is faith. You have to believe that a miracle is possible for you. There are some who can celebrate in the miracles and successes of others, but don't really believe that God can change *their* situation. If you have enough faith to believe in the possibilities of miracles, God will open the world of possibilities of deliverance for you. Paul says, *"Without faith, it is impossible to please God, for he that cometh to God must first believe that he is a rewarder of them that diligently seek him."* [1]

Before you pray another prayer, you've got to believe that God can answer the ones that you have already prayed. Before you begin another fast, you've got to believe that He is able to do what you have asked Him to do. *God is not a man that he should lie, or the son of man that he should repent.*[2] If you can believe God and speak a word of deliverance before you see the manifestation, He will step in. It's all about your faith. Your possibilities hinge on your faith. Other people cannot speak possibilities in your life. Jesus looked at a poor and sick woman and told her that her faith made her whole.

The disciples around Him didn't have enough faith to believe that one fragile old woman could touch His garment, and He would dry up the blood disease in her body. What about you? Do you have enough faith to leave the house, even if you have to crawl down the street and others have to trample on you while you are trying to get in touch with Jesus? If you can touch the hem of His garment, you too shall be made whole.

Paul says, "Now faith..." This is not yesterday's faith but right now faith. You need your own faith. You may have enough faith to come out, but do you have enough faith to go through? *"Now faith is the substance of things that are hoped for, but the evidence of things that are not seen."* [3] Faith is the belief of what you have not seen, and trusting in what you cannot prove. When I tell people that I am blessed, they want to know how many stocks and bonds I have and if I have paid off my mortgage. I may not be able to prove it, but I just believe that it is already done. I've got enough faith to look at what has not yet happened and claim it as already done. Before you see it, you can believe in advance because it's already done.

Several years ago, my family and I were sitting in the hospital. My father was in critical condition. I prayed a prayer, asking for something limited. I did not have enough faith to ask for what I thought was impossible. I asked God to allow my father to live long enough for us to celebrate one more Father's Day. God answered my prayer and allowed him to live more than three years. God showed me that He could do exceeding abundantly more than I could ask or think. Do you have faith to ask for the impossible, faith to expect the unbelievable, faith to walk in the miraculous? Do you have enough faith to do what Peter did - leave the boat and walk on water? If you begin to sink, you can cry out, "Jesus, save me!" Do you have enough faith to walk in the possibilities of life? Have you been praying for a difficult situation?

You know that some people don't think you can make it. It looks like everything is stacked against you. Can you believe before you see that God is able to make a way out of no way? Can you praise God in advance? Charge your next praise! Put it on credit. Go to work tomorrow morning and act as if you have a promotion. Strut your stuff. When they ask you what is going on, tell them that you are anticipating a blessing. Do you have enough faith to shake your finger in the enemy's face, knowing that what he meant for evil, God is going to turn that situation around for good? Do you have to see it to believe it, or do you have a feeling that everything is going to be all right?

Brother Thomas Didymus doubted the Resurrection of Jesus. He heard about the resurrection, but he had not seen the evidence. For some, all you need in order to hold on to hope is a Word from the Lord. You are still sick; you are still broke, but you are holding on to His Word. God says that He will return unto you the years that the adversary took from you. You may not know what is going on in your family, but you have a Word from the Lord that says your seed shall be blessed. God has given you His Word that He would never leave you or forsake you. Don't allow doubt to rob you of your hope. Thomas, on the other hand, needed to see Jesus for himself. Eight days later, Jesus walked through the door and had Thomas touch His hand and his side. Then, Thomas instantly believed! Having seen Jesus, Thomas said, *"My Lord and my God."* [4] Jesus was not impressed, because Thomas called Him Lord and God *after* seeing Him. On the other side of the door is your blessing. Do you have enough faith to believe before He walks through the door? God is not impressed with how you shout *after* you get delivered. If you want to impress God, have a praise on your lips even though you've been laid off from work, having had someone break your heart, *still* have joy.

Have you ever been so sick that you could hardly raise your head off your pillow, yet in your sickness, you found a way to praise God? Jesus told Thomas that he believed in Him because of what he had seen. Can you give God your best praise on your worst days? Jesus said to Thomas, blessed are they who have not seen but yet believe. Do you qualify for a special blessing? In spite of what you cannot see, Jesus is on the other side of the door getting ready to walk through it. Have faith in God.

CHAPTER SIXTEEN

Will You Go Where You Have Not Been?

Now the LORD had said unto Abram, Get thee out of thy country, and from thy kindred, and from thy father's house, unto a land that I will shew thee: And I will make of thee a great nation, and I will bless thee, and make thy name great; and thou shalt be a blessing: And I will bless them that bless thee, and curse him that curseth thee: and in thee shall all families of the earth be blessed. So Abram departed, as the LORD had spoken unto him; and Lot went with him:

Genesis 12:1-4a

By faith Abraham, when he was called to go out into a place which he should after receive for an inheritance, obeyed; and he went out, not knowing whither he went. By faith he sojourned in the land of promise, as [in] a strange country, dwelling in tabernacles with Isaac and Jacob, the heirs with him of the same promise:

Hebrews 11:8-9

Has God ever asked you to do a difficult thing? Has God ever asked you to do something that you have never done before, all the while knowing that He never said to you, "Here is the proof that you can do it"? Has He ever asked you to leave

125

where you are or to change courses? Is God challenging you to do something different? It may be a career move. It may be a personal challenge in your life. It may be something concerning your faith. It may be something concerning your church home. Has God asked you to do something purely on faith, to leave that which is familiar, that which is solid? Has he asked you to go someplace or to do something that you did not know about, something that you did not know how it would turn out? Has God asked you to take a risk, to trust Him?

Abram is a great example of an individual whom God challenged to do something that was pretty difficult. God challenged him to do something that was highly unusual. Prior to God manifesting Himself to Israel as the chosen generation, biblical text will tell you that Abram lived with the Chaldeans. He lived in a secular humanistic society, which had literally forgotten about their God. They had forgotten about the God that made Adam and Eve, the God of the flood, the God of Noah. *Now the LORD had said unto Abram, Get thee out of thy country, and from thy kindred, and from thy father's house, unto a land that I will shew thee: And I will make of thee a great nation, and I will bless thee, and make thy name great; and thou shalt be a blessing: And I will bless them that bless thee, and curse him that curseth thee: and in thee shall all families of the earth be blessed. So Abram departed, as the LORD had spoken unto him; and Lot went with him: and Abram was seventy and five years old when he departed out of Haran.*[1]

God challenged Abram, even though he did not have a long-lasting relationship with God. He wasn't the father of Israel yet. He was the son of a Chaldean. One day, God spoke to him and told him to leave his country. He had to leave his relatives. He had to leave his father's house. Abram was comfortable where he was. He had nothing to worry about. He was around people he knew: people who looked like him and acted like him, until the day God changed everything. God said to Abram, "Get out of your country, away from your kindred, and leave your father's house unto a land that I will show you." Did you grasp that? *"A land that I will show you," God said.* That is big-time faith. God did not say to Abram, "There's land that is plush with milk and honey and all of these things are going to be there...." God said, "Go there, and when you go there, I will make you great." There was nothing to substantiate what God said to him other than God's word. Will you trust God the way Abram trusted God? God promised Abram to make of him a great nation. Abram was not there yet.

At that point, Abram was nobody. Abram had no biological offspring. He had one nephew, Lot, who had all kinds of problems. Lot became more of a headache that an asset. The first chance Lot got, he stabbed Abram in the back. Lot took the best land and left his uncle the worst land. Here is a young man whom Abraham had raised, and this is how Lot treated him. There are some around you who will mistreat you for their own selfish gain. Most people are selfish. It's the basic nature of people. We all look out for our own self-interest. That's how we do it. There is a little bit of Lot in all of us. Abraham brought Lot to the land and gave him a choice. There was green pasture on one side and hilly land on the other side. Lot chose the best. He did not look out for his uncle. Lot pitched his tent towards Sodom and Gomorrah. Abraham took the rough part. As it turned out, Abraham had to come and rescue Lot from what he thought was a blessing. Be careful whom you mistreat. That same person may have to come snatch you out of destruction.

God promised to bless Abram and make his name great, and He promised that he would be a blessing. He promised to bless them that blessed him and to curse them that curse him. His promise was that in Abraham all the families of the earth should be blessed. At that time all Abram had from God was a word. So Abram departed as the Lord had spoken to him, although he did not know where he was going. Neither did he know what he was going to do when he got there. All he knew was that God told him to do something. Abraham was called by God to go out. The Bible makes it clear that Abram had left because he was called by God. Be sure that God has called you, and don't try to step out on your own calling. Make sure you have the right calling. There are too many people who think that they have been called by God, and the enemy has enticed them to do something that they know they are not ready to do. You'd think if God called you, he would straighten you up. You want to be mightily used by God, and you are the biggest gossip and backbiter in your community. Every time something goes wrong, you are in the midst of the mess, and yet you want God to elevate you.

God is not that desperate that He has to use someone who is not willing to change for Him. You have to be called by God. You want the challenge and the reward before you make the step of faith. God wants to bless you after you have enough faith to leave what is familiar and travel down a road where you do not know where you are going. After you leave then, will God give you an inheritance? You also have to obey God. Abram went out without knowing where he was going. Now, you know his kin talked about him. Abram did not have to go get confirmation from his father or his family. The challenge was not a family affair. It was a personal affair. Are you waiting for confirmation over things that God said to you about you? If Abram had gone to his father, his father might not have allowed him to go, because his father would not have understood. Abram knew what God had said to him.

Are there some people, places, and things in your life that you should have left a long time ago? Why haven't you? It is a difficult thing to do, isn't it? And yet, it is very easy to tell other people what they should do. One of the best times of my life was when I was an assistant pastor at Bible Way. I could make all kinds of recommendations and didn't have to worry about the consequences. I threw out all kinds of radical and wild ideas. The difference is that the assistant makes the recommendations, but the top leader makes the decisions. It's very easy to make recommendations about other people's lives, because it doesn't always involve you, but what do you do when you become the captain of your own ship? You have to make recommendations about your own life and your family's lives, and that's when the magnitude of the responsibility hits home, doesn't it?

You may be comfortable doing what you are doing and don't want the Lord to ask you to do anything else. You don't want to be asked to take a leadership position in your community. You don't want to work with ministries. You just want to attend church, pay your tithes, go home, and not give an account to anyone. There is no accountability. What will happen if God changes all of that? Is God calling you to a higher level of responsibility? Does God want to put more on you? What if He asks you to do something for His Kingdom?

In order for you to do it, you must venture into territory that is not familiar. You may have to leave what you know behind as well as leave your friends. The people you used to be with cannot be with you in this new dimension of your life. Are you willing to leave what's familiar behind? Are you willing to let God be your friend, walk with you, and talk with you? Go ahead and build your ark on dry land. Do what God has asked you to do and forget about what people are saying. I'm talking about risk-takers. There are too many scared Christians.

Too many people are stuck where they are because they are not willing to venture out.

They are not willing to lose some things. They are not willing to lose their reputations. They are not willing to be used by God. Are you willing to lose everything? Are you willing to take a risk? God wants us to step out on faith. Change the neighborhood around you. Why can't we build pharmacies? Why can't we build senior citizens' homes? Why can't we turn abandoned buildings into dream centers? God has told me that if I ever lost my boldness to step out on faith, my ministry would suffer severely. He will bring in someone new who will take a chance and be willing to say, "Here I am Lord." God is challenging some of you to take a chance.

By faith, Abram journeyed to a land of promise in a strange country. He went to a new land based on a promise, and he did not even know how blessed it was. Abraham had no children. He had no sons. All he had was his stubborn nephew, Lot, who was with him. The blessings that God has for you are the things that other people can't see. But the promise of God is somewhere locked up inside of you, and God said that if you are willing to dwell in tabernacles, then even in your temporary dwelling place, there is a blessing in you. Somewhere between where you left and where you are going to end up, God has already placed an Isaac and a Jacob in you. You just can't see it. You can't feel it. Isaac was already there; Abraham just didn't know it. No wonder when the angel said to Sarah that

131

she was going to give birth to a child, she laughed. Sarah gave birth to Isaac at 90 years old, and Abraham was 100 years old when Isaac was born. *"Trust in the Lord. Lean not unto your own understanding. In all thy ways, acknowledge Him."* [2] Somewhere in you is your promised blessing. Your dream house is already in you. The job is already in you. The relationship is already in you. You are walking around in tabernacles, carrying your blessing. One day, God is going to allow the blessing to be birthed out of you. That's why at 90 years old, Sarah could give birth to a child. It wasn't about Sarah. It was about God's promise to Abraham. He may not come when you want Him, but He is always on time. Even in your current state, your promised blessing is with you. Keep going. Watch God make a way out of no way. If God promised it, God will do just what He said.

CHAPTER SEVENTEEN

Will You Speak What You Cannot Prove?

So she went and came unto the man of God to Mount Carmel. And it came to pass, when the man of God saw her afar off, that he said to Gehazi his servant, Behold, [yonder is] that Shunammite: Run now, I pray thee, to meet her, and say unto her, Is it well with thee? Is it well with thy husband? Is it well with the child? And she answered, It is well.

2 Kings 4:25-26

...and calleth those things which be not as though they were.

Romans 4:17(b)

Do you know that you can speak the things that you are entitled to have? When God says that He will give you the desires of your heart, He assumes that your heart is right. Otherwise, you would literally take things literally that do not apply to your situation, and come up with all kinds of erroneous assumptions.

Don't try to give a theological opinion out of what doesn't apply. That's why you must study to show yourself approved. Rightly divide the word. God has challenged us to have "say it faith."

133

There comes a time in your life in which your faith will be defined by what you are able to say out of your mouth, without having the evidence in your hand. That's called "faith." There are times in which your conscience will tell you not to say it, because it will make you look ridiculous. Your faith, however, will say, "Claim it anyhow." Things appear to be one way, but you are speaking not as they are, but as you know they are going to be. I suggest that you write the three words, "it is well" down and keep them with you. Every time the enemy tries to confront you with negativity, say, "It is well." When the evidence is not there to verify it, still say, "It is well." If you only speak what the evidence dictates, you are not a faith walker; you are a scientist. Scientists need evidence, whereas faith walkers say things that they hope to be but cannot yet prove.

God is saying to us that we need to speak some things that have not yet been manifested as if they were. If you are not yet in life where you are going to be, you can still say, "I am blessed." Although you are financially challenged, you can still say, "I am blessed." Those who are not feeling well in their bodies can still say, "It is well." Even if it never happens, your faith will still have been demonstrated. Shadrach, Meshach, and Abed-Nego said to King Nebuchadnezzar that even if God did not deliver them, they wanted him to know with a surety that God was still able to do it. That took faith. It took faith to look into the face of a fiery furnace and still declare that God was able to deliver them. Faith is speaking what you cannot prove. Not all of it has to be spoken in the presence of other people.

I am convinced that we sometimes say things in the presence of other people that we don't believe ourselves. We call that perpetrating. The Bible calls such people hypocrites, people who just talk the religious jargon and don't believe it. They will say it in church, or they will say it because someone has asked them to say it, but their lives do not reflect that they believe what they just uttered. If you believe that God can work things out on your behalf, you will not be crying to everyone who calls you on the phone. You would have stopped complaining a long time ago if you knew that God was able to do what He promised.

Throughout the Bible, God puts a particular interest in what we say and how we say it and what comes out of our mouths. Some 628 times in the Bible, God uses the word "speak." God wants you to understand that deliverance can come out of what you believe and what you are able to say. *"If you say unto this mountain be thou removed and cast into the sea and don't doubt it in your heart, it shall be done."* [1] Even if you look at the principles of salvation, the book of Romans tells us that if we confess with our mouths the Lord Jesus and believe it in our hearts that God raised Him from the dead, we shall be saved. That's why I appreciate baptism.

It is your personal identification with the greatest act of human history - the death, burial, and resurrection of Jesus Christ. Baptism doesn't save you -salvation comes by faith alone. But baptism is your personal testimony to, and the inward assurance of, your passage from the old life to the new life. In other words, it is an outward symbol of an inward commitment.

If deeds saved you, people would be saved without making a personal commitment on their own. If dipping you in the water saved you, you would have gotten your kids in the water a long time ago! Every week, you would be dipping them in the water, if all it took was water to get them where they needed to be, but it takes more than that. It takes a repentant heart and a changed heart, and it takes a confession out of your mouth. The Bible assumes that the mouth confesses what the heart believes. If the heart believes that Jesus Christ is your Savior, then the mouth will say it. That's why He says if you confess with your mouth and believe with your heart, you will be saved. Throughout the pages of the gospel, Jesus has always said to people that it is important to understand that what you say means as much as what you do. When the disciples were going to the temple and saw the man who was lame, they asked of him, and he asked for alms. The disciples told him that they had neither silver nor gold but declared, *"In the name of Jesus, take up your bed and walk."* [2] In other words, what you have asked for may not be what you need. What would have happened if the disciples had given him silver and gold? He would have still been lame. That's why we should confess and ask God not just for the things we know we can get, but also for the things for which there is no evidence that they can happen. You just need to believe that the God you serve is able to do it. Every now and then, you should have enough faith to utter some private words to God about what you expect God to do in your life. God is holding on to the blessings you lost, and when He gives it back to you, He is going to return it to you with interest!

Let us consider Job. Job just had a dialogue with his three so-called friends, friends who came to judge him. They sat in Job's house, ate his food, and proceeded to tell him why he was going through so much turmoil. Yet the Lord turned the captivity of Job when Job prayed for his friends. You see, when you can ask God to bless the person who has "hurt" you the most, God will turn it around. When you can get hurt in the house of a friend, turn around, and pray for the person who hurt you, God will bless you. There is a reason why the word "when" is placed in the scripture. The latter could not have been until the former occurred.

In other words, if Job had never prayed for those no-good buddies of his, maybe God would have never turned things around in his life. God is getting ready to bless you when you turn loose of your anger and your hurts. You must let go of it. God can't give you new blessings when you are still holding onto some old hurts. Forget about what they did to you. It is not about them. It is about *your* peace, *your* deliverance, and *your* prosperity. The Lord gave Job dividends. If you know anything about investments, a dividend is not what you put in, but an amount *above* what you put in. *"And God gave to Job twice as much as he had before. Then came there unto him all his brethren and all his sisters, and all they then had been of his acquaintance before and did eat bread with him in his house... and comforted him.*"[3] Consider all the evil that had been brought to him, all the people who got up in his face, ate his food, and took up his time. God sent them away, and when they came back, God made them give Job what they had.

I want to help you understand something here: Just in case you want to praise them for their generous acts, know that they had no choice. God gave Job twice as much as his friends had given him combined. It means that God touched their hearts and made them give up their possessions and give them to Job. The same Job whom they criticized, they turned around and blessed. The Lord blessed the latter Job more than the beginning Job. In other words, he ended up with more than he started out with. You have to understand that Job had to keep the faith between the time that he lost everything and the time he got it back. Look at all the times in scripture that Job spoke positively. In all of this, Job never cursed God. You must be able to speak some things and believe some things between when God is getting ready to bless you and when you are going through something. You have to have enough faith to believe that God will do what He said He would do. You have to speak it. You have to say it even if you cannot prove it.

CHAPTER EIGHTEEN

Will You Sing Your Song in a Strange Land?

By the rivers of Babylon, there we sat down, yea, we wept, when we remembered Zion. We hanged our harps upon the willows in the midst thereof. For there they that carried us away captive required of us a song; and they that wasted us required of us mirth, saying, Sing us one of the songs of Zion. How shall we sing the LORD'S song in a strange land?

Psalm 137:1-4

When the Assyrians invaded Jerusalem, they carried away the brightest and the smartest, and those with the greatest potential, so that they could use them for their services. They captured the prominent young people in those towns and cities. It was equivalent to someone invading the city and taking away those who had the greatest potential to do wonderful things while they were still in the prime of their lives. They invaded their land and led them into captivity. The enemies of Judah came in and invaded their territory. They took them to a place called Babylon, a strange land. What is ironic is that Babylon is now modern-day Iraq. The people who were in captivity called their place of bondage a "strange land." They were probably thinking, "We are not from here. These are not our people. We do not know them. We don't want to be here. We are not here because of our choice although we were made to praise God; you are asking us to sing songs in a strange land."

It is easy to sing your song and give your testimony when you are around familiar people who do what you do and who understand why you do what you do. But what happens when your place changes and your circumstances are different? Your real test of faith is not how you respond when you are in a familiar setting and sitting by people who you know. How would you handle it if your circumstances change? Will you be the same or will you reserve what you do only for the right setting?

Until you can take what you do outside of your familiar environment and go beyond that, you are not where you should be. That is why God challenges us and tells us that our greatness is going to be determined by how we respond to changes in circumstances. A strange land is what you go through when you are hurt, wounded, depressed, and broke, with no one to lean on. You are having a valley experience: a strange land. What happens when your money runs out and the one you loved walks out, and the things you love break down or wear out, and you have nothing left?

The disciples said to Jesus on the mountaintop, *"It is good for us to be here."* [1] They wanted to build a tabernacle and stay there. Jesus rebuked them, because at the foot of the mountain, there was a lunatic boy who needed Jesus. Peter, James, and John wanted to stay on the mountain so that they would not have to face the valley. Your greatest work will be in the valley. You need to be able to minister to those who are in Babylon. Can you still say the God you serve is still able to do what he said he could do when you are sick and hurting?

Babylon is not a place of your own choosing, but a place of your destiny. In other words, if it were up to you, you would not have chosen to go there. God wants you to go there because in Babylon, your character is refined. Until you have gone through the fire, you don't know what it is to stand up and say, "God, here I am." Until you have been through some hard times and high waters, you have not arrived. Sometimes it is not an issue of doing what we were meant to do; sometimes it is an issue of whether we can do it when we are not where we want to be. In other words, can you be what you were meant to be in a place where you don't want to be? As long as you are in a place where you want to be, you can praise, you can be a worshiper, you can be a missionary. You can be a prayer warrior, as long as you are with other prayer warriors, but can you go to people who can't talk like you? Can you go to people who are 100 percent "street-minded"?

God's Word was meant to strengthen believers so that you will be the evangelical tool to let your light shine before men, so that they may see your good work and glorify God. Some of you are too religious. You quote too many scriptures.

You are in church too often. If you are really going to make a difference, you have to go out into darkness. Light shining to light is irrelevant. Darkness cannot comprehend light. Light needs to shine among darkness. Turn your flashlight off from shining it in the light and shine it at midnight. I am not impressed with flashlights shining in the day. Move beyond that. Don't be like those who could only praise God when the situation was right. *"How can we sing the songs of Zion in a strange land?"* [2]

You may be traveling through Babylon. You may have lost your job. The one you love with all you heart may leave you. People you rely on may let you down, but how you respond when things are not going your way will determine what God has for you in the end. Let your songs of praise be consistent before the Lord. Make sure that your praise is not predicated on your circumstances. If your circumstances change, you should still be able to sing your song, even in a strange land.

Chapter Nineteen

The Power in You

But ye shall receive power, after that the Holy Ghost is come upon you: and ye shall be witnesses unto me both in Jerusalem, and in all Judaea, and in Samaria, and unto the uttermost part of the earth.

Acts 1:8

Now unto him that is able to do exceeding abundantly above all that we ask or think, according to the power that worketh in us.

Ephesians 3:20

I am convinced that you will never understand and appreciate your possibilities until you understand and appreciate your purpose. I am also convinced that discovering your purpose is not enough. Doing something about what you have been called to do is what God expects. It is essential that you walk in possibilities. I have discovered that as long as people feel that it is God's power at work, it lets them off the hook. They feel that they have no control. It is not just God's power at work, but also the power within you. If you are going to be delivered, if you are going to be over-comers, you need power in you. It is the power that is in you that will determine your destiny.

It is the power within you that will open up your possibilities. Being around God is not enough. The thief comes to steal, to kill, and to destroy. You've got to withstand the adversary. It is not enough for you to walk in His presence and then walk out the door without His power dwelling in you. So many people like being spectators. I call it the "fan mentality." You stand in the stands, waving your pompoms. You've got to face the adversary for yourself. You need real power. You need something to keep you from doing what you want to do.

The disciples of Jesus are an example for us to review. Something happened to them that made their lives different when they received the indwelling of the Holy Spirit. For three and a half years, the disciples were around Jesus. When they were hungry, He divided the fish and the loaves. When they needed to pay their taxes, they reached their hands into the mouth of the fish and God provided resources. When their family members were sick, He healed them. They were dependent on the presence of Jesus. That is why when they went to the other side of the sea and a storm arose, they cried out for Jesus to help them. He was right there in the boat and yet they cried out to Him. They were so dependent on Jesus doing everything for them that they did not grow. Hanging out near power doesn't give you power. In spite of the fact that they were in the presence of the Messiah, their lives were a mess.

I have discovered that some of the most troubled people I have ever seen in my life are church people. Some of them are the biggest liars, whoremongers, and backstabbers; they are the ones who hang around the presence of God. God's presence may thrill you, but it won't fill you. I want the thrill and the fill! The thrill makes you feel good at the event. That is why Peter said, "It is good for us to be here" [1] while he was on Mount Transfiguration, yet he could not cast out demons from a boy who was possessed down in the valley. Jesus had twelve men who were weak-kneed, lying, backstabbing, and doubting, for three and a half years. Fifty days after the resurrection, a change came. Jesus was not only around them, but also in them.

In order to get what God has for you, you must lock down and lock out everything else. The disciples had to get over who would sit on the right or left of Jesus. For ten days, they cried, prayed, and worshiped God. You see, the power is not around you or above you, but it is *in* you. When you are filled with the Holy Spirit, you have power to tell the enemy to get behind you. King David said, *"Thou preparest a table before me in the presence of mine enemies: thou anointest my head with oil."* [2] There is something about the Holy Spirit that you can't explain. God can do exceeding, abundantly more than you can ask or think according to the power that is in you.

You have the power to stop the adversary in his tracks. You have the power to declare that never again will you go down the same destructive path. You need a breakthrough in your life. You have the power to speak to the mountains. You have the power to walk through the furnace of fire and praise

God in the midst of the fire. You've got the power to do what God has asked you to do. If you are going to change where you are, there has to be a power that works in you. The problem is that too many times we expect outward manifestations of what God is going to do. We fail to realize that the greatest growth in our spiritual lives come from within. It's not the unknown language that you speak, but the language you speak that is known and heard by other people.

Sometimes it takes the Holy Spirit in you to be calm when others have tested your patience. Anyone can blow off steam and get things off his or her chest. We are human, and there are times we lose it; none of us are perfect. The difference in someone with the Holy Spirit is that if you lose it, you go back and get it. You don't walk around for a year, insulting people. That is not godly, and that behavior will do nothing but hurt you. It's not a matter of personalities. Have you not changed as a result of knowing God? If you were quick to react before you were saved, and you still can't bridle your tongue or check your emotions, then ask yourself, are you saved? Was there no change in your life? Salvation saves you from the inside out. Don't expect "exceeding abundantly" without the power.

One of the things that stands out about the disciples is that for three and a half years, they were in the presence of the Messiah, and it really did not change their lives. We have to be mindful that going to church alone won't do it. They were in the presence of the King of Kings, but when they saw a chance to backstab each other, they did. Thomas doubted; Judas stole; Peter denied. The others ran away. They had three and a half years in His presence, but nothing happened. You will not get deliverance in your life until you invite Him in. You are such a good person and you mean so well, but your life won't change until God is invited in by you.

There is a different level of readiness for His presence than His indwelling. God's presence can co-exist just about anywhere. But His indwelling can only coexist in a temple that is ready. God will not put new wine in old wineskins. You are known by the spirit that comes out of you. When you carry the spirit of your father, you will act like your father. Paul says, *"Let this mind be in you, which was also in Christ Jesus."* [3] In order to get this mindset, God won't force it on you. The first word in this scripture is "let." You have to accept it. You have to invite God's spirit in. Let it take over your life. The only way for it to happen is for you to open the door. People cannot pray the Holy Spirit in you. If that were the case, we would have prayed a long time ago. If you invite Him in, your life becomes a living epistle, and others will want what you have.

As a result of the inward power of God, three things will occur:

1. You become a person who unites, not divides.
2. The Holy Spirit will give you courage to stand up with

boldness and say, "For God I live, and for God I will die." God is working on your transformation from the inside out.

3. You become anointed. If you are ever going to get there, it has to start from the inside out. Ask God to change you from the inside out. When you are put to a test, you will understand that God has done it for a reason. Ask God for the infilling of His spirit. Do you hear the Lord knocking? Will you open the door? Will you let Him in?

CHAPTER TWENTY

When the Brook Dries Up

And it came to pass after a while, that the brook dried up, because there had been no rain in the land. And the barrel of meal wasted not, neither did the cruse of oil fail, according to the word of the LORD, which he spake by Elijah.

1 Kings 17:7, 16

All of us get to the point in our lives when we don't know what to do, what to trust, or what to believe. Our backs are flat against the wall. When someone gets to that point, the church needs to evangelize by going where the people are. They are not in some ecclesiastical, theological, or spiritual place where you can impress them with your intellect. They need help. There are people who are drowning. They need a life raft. They don't need somebody quoting scripture to them on how to build a boat. They need a hand right now. I've been in that place, where I just needed God to deliver me. What we don't know is that our greatest opportunities happen after we go through certain stages in our lives. God says that conditions will change. Look at Job.

He was once the richest man in the land who feared God and shunned evil. Yet the messenger of doom delivered to Job news that changed his condition overnight.[1] Have you been there? Do you know others who have never gone through what you went through, yet they give their ten cents' worth of advice? They can't understand why you didn't put money away. Perhaps you didn't have any money to put away. Perhaps you did not anticipate losing your job. Perhaps you did not anticipate someone walking out on you. Perhaps you didn't think you would get sick and be laid off without being compensated for three months. Situations in your life will change, and you cannot anticipate them all. Even if you anticipate some things, other things start to happen. That is when the brook dries up.

All of us will have times in our lives when our conditions change. Even good people weep at night. Change is coming. Get ready for the change. Not only change for the good, but there are times in everyone's life when things change for worse. Situations may come in your life where you have no control over what's happening. The last time I checked, you could not control the rain. The brook dries up when there was no rain. Elijah had nothing to do with the fact that the brook dried up. Things just happened.

It doesn't mean that you are not "prayed up." I get so frustrated with people who are "holier than thou" and they like to rub it in your face at your worst hour. Everyone has a scripture and a revelation for you when you are at rock bottom.

Rarely does a person want you to quote scriptures to him or her in such a moment as that. Can you just put your arms around that person and tell him or her that you love them? You can't be spiritual all the time. One of the greatest weapons of the enemy is to get us on a mountain and delude us to think that we are greater than anyone else. We begin to think that we have a word of spirituality for every situation.

There are some situations when there is no word, nothing that can be said. I believe that at some point you have been right there. You may be saved, yet you are in a tough situation. Now, not only did your conditions change because of circumstances beyond your control, but even the provisions that you had are not in your control. Elijah was fed by ravens. He did not plow the field. He didn't pick the corn. He didn't prepare any meals. He ate because God gave him his daily bread. You may be sitting by the brook right now, and you are living the good life. The only reason you are where you are is because God has blessed you, not that you have done it by yourself.

Do you know that all of your provisions come from the Creator? Everything you have is a result of God. It is because of God that we move, breathe, and have our being. It is because of God that we have a job, even if it is not a perfect job. If it were up to the adversary, we would not have anything. I thank God that all of my good days are a result of what He has done. You should not take credit when times are good, because they are not good because you have been good. You may have been living on grace and mercy. Elijah was fed by grace and mercy. When God allowed the brook to dry up, Elijah never complained, because he knew he had nothing to do with it. You beat up on yourselves too much. It's not your fault. You may be going through situations, and you are blaming yourself.

It is not your fault. You cannot control the rain. Sometimes the brook just dries up. When conditions change, people sometimes act foolish. You are trying to figure out what you have done. You think that you should have lost more weight. Maybe you should have worked three jobs…No! No! No! It's not your fault. Some of you have been crying too often, and God wants you to know that it is not your fault. The brook just dried up. Elijah got up and went to the city of Zarephath, and God had commanded a widow woman to sustain him. God was changing his condition. God doesn't want you to worry about when your brook dries up. He is the God of provision. Have you ever lost a job, only to get a better job? Have you ever been broken-hearted, just to be set up with your destined relationship? God had to move you from here in order to get you there. You should thank Him for the transformation. You should thank the Lord for uprooting you from your safety zone and taking you somewhere you did not understand. God is about to change your situation. Do not lose your faith because God is able. The enemy may have been lying to you by telling you it's your fault. The enemy is a liar. God is going to liberate you. God is getting ready to set you up for a destiny blessing.

Temporal blessings make you feel good for a moment. Destiny blessings, however, will bless you the rest of your life.

There was a widow woman who had a temporal blessing. All she had left before she died was the handful of meal that she was going to make before she died. Had she refused to give her last meal to a stranger who in turn blessed her, she would have felt good for one more night before she died. Temporal blessings will not last. God was ready to set the woman up for a destiny blessing. Because of her faith and obedience, her barrel of meal never ran out. How do you get a destiny blessing? Give up temporal things. If you hold on to what is temporal, you will never get what you are destined to have. This woman gave up what was temporal, and God gave her what she was destined to have. She gave up more than a meal.

She was sowing a seed. You, too, are going to reap what you sow. Why won't you sow seeds of praise? Some people are holding onto their seed and will die with their seed. You have to turn it loose. You can have a crop if you part with the seed and put it in the ground. Let rain and dirt come on it. Let the sun shine on it. It has to be fertilized. God will turn a temporal blessing into a blessed future. God has given you your destiny blessing. When you receive destiny blessings, the next house you move into will be bigger than you desire. You will never have to move again; your next job will be your destiny job. You will never feel alone again. God is about to change some things in your life. There is a change in the atmosphere. Receive your change.

Oftentimes in life, our greatest opportunities happen as a result of our worst crises. Knowing this changes the way you look at a crisis. If you can look at a crisis as an opportunity to bless you, then you look at that thing that was going to destroy you as something that is going to enhance your life. It's a matter of perspective. As a result, you are better. If you had not lifted the weights, you would not be as strong as you are now. The way to gain strength is through resistance. The more resistance you endure, the stronger you become.

You can't get your blessings until you overcome resistance. You may have weights on your shoulder. Resistance training will help you become stronger. People tend to shun resistance because it is hard, but sometime it's necessary. Often times your crisis is your resistance. Sometimes God will have a weight on you so that you can run this race with patience. If you want to get somewhere in life, you've got to be disciplined enough to come through the difficult times. Lift that resistance. Push your way through it. The brook drying up symbolizes the time when conditions that are beyond our control change. It's not your fault that there is no rain. You can't control whether people gossip about you. You can't control whether they dislike you. Some people will dislike you just because of who you are, and they will bring turmoil to your life, when all you have done is what God has told you to do. Some people are just diabolical, hateful people.

Elijah was being fed by the ravens by the brook, but conditions changed for him. The rain stopped and the brook dried up, so there was no more food for him to eat. That was a crisis in his life. What are you going to do when situations beyond your control happen, when you don't know what to do because you are in a situation that is more than you can handle? In some situations, things happen outside of your control. In other situations, things happen to you that are more than you can handle. They get too heavy. You can't do it by yourself. You need help in order to get to the next level, and your prayer becomes, "Lord, if you don't intervene, I'm not going to make it."

When you are weightlifting, you have spotters. A spotter is someone who stands by your side while you lift, in case the weights get too heavy. Have you ever gotten to the point that you could not get past the last lift, and God had to lift you the rest of the way? God will never put anything on you that you cannot handle, but in all ways, He will give you a way to escape.[2] When you get to the point where you cannot handle it, God will step in. Thank God for His assistance during your resistance. Have you ever nearly lost your mind? Just before the breakdown, God stepped in and sent a breakthrough.

God only showed up in the fiery furnace after the Hebrew boys were already in there. You have to have enough faith to be willing to step in and believe that before you are consumed, God will step in right on time. When you have lifted all you can, God will take the burden off you. Before God takes you out of the fire, He will walk around with you. Before He brings you out of your situation, in the midst of your hardship, God will rejoice with you. Both of these situations are somewhat common in our Christian walk.

Expect the brook to dry up. Expect there to be times in which you don't know what to do. *"There hath no temptation taken you but such as is common to man...."* [3] What you are going through is not unusual. You are not unique because you are going through situations as you are. I believe that everyone who commits his or her life to this Christian journey will have to walk this road at some point in his or her life. Get ready for your brook to dry up. Get ready for your back to be against the wall. If you aren't there, get ready for it. If you have not been there yet, get ready for it, and if you have been there, get ready for it again. The Bible says that Satan left Jesus for a season; he's coming back. But what he got the first time will be waiting for him again. Greater is He that is within you than He that is in the world.

There are three things you should remember as you go through your experiences:

1. Sometimes provisions can come through unusual sources. There are some situations in which you look at people and think that they can do nothing for you. Be

156

careful how you entertain strangers, because you may be entertaining angels unaware. The source of Elijah's blessings in I Kings came through a widowed woman who had nothing. So many times, you look for Prince Charming on a horse to save you, and you turn your nose up at others. What you need to know is that the Messiah rode in on a borrowed donkey. You may have a lot of people riding on their high horses, but they are not for you. Be careful, because the source of your blessings can come through the person you least expect. That's why you have to wait to see what God has to say in your situation. Who would send a hungry prophet to a hungry, widowed woman with only one handful of meal? That does not make sense. People who are financially broke don't go to other people who are also financially broke get money. It takes God to send you to someone in worse shape than you are in. Your next blessing may come from someone who has less than you do. We often group people into categories of who we think can and cannot bless us. The person you think will be a blessing to you may just be worse off than you think.

2. Sometimes your enemies can bring you closer to the Lord. As a result of the enemies of Jehoshaphat, he called for a fast and gathered all Judah into the heart of the city, and they began to pray in the middle of the

day because the enemies were on their tracks. Those who bring the greatest amount of trouble just drive you closer into the arms of God. If they had not dogged you out, you would not be where you are today. What the enemy meant for evil, God meant for good. Are you now closer to God because of what others did to you? They thought that they were hurting you, but what they did drove you into the arms of the Lord. As a result of what they put you through, you have a more intimate relationship with God. The person who contributed to King David's life more than anyone else was Saul. It was Saul who drove King David out of his comfort zone. It was Saul's javelin that drove King David into the caves and into the valley. If David had never gone through the valley, he would not have written, "...*Yea though I walk through the valley of the shadows of death, I will fear no evil...*" [4] If he never went through anything, he would have never experienced goodness and mercy.

3. Sometimes the best thing to do when you don't know what to do is nothing. God wants you to wait on Him. Keep your mouth shut. Stay put. Don't say a word. Even if someone is trying to destroy you, do nothing. Stand still. If you need to do something, then do what you were made to do. Praise God. When you feel like retaliating, don't do it. Instead, just praise God. When the brook dries up and you don't know what to do,

stand still. While you are praising God, He is ambushing your enemies. Through your waiting, God is working out your provision. If you praise God, He will fight for you. He will not forget your labor of love.

Chapter Twenty-One

When You Don't Know What to Do

O our God, wilt thou not judge them? For we have no might against this great company that cometh against us; neither know we what to do: but our eyes are upon thee.

2 Chronicles 20:12

Some of our greatest opportunities and possibilities will come after some of our most difficult times. That's how God operates. After we have gone through what we consider to be the worst times in our lives, God seems to send us the greatest opportunities and the greatest possibilities. In the last chapter, we talked about when the brook dries up. The brook represents situations that are changing in our lives. These changes often happen beyond our control. Sometimes things happen in your life beyond your control. The prophet Elijah could not control the rain, and the brook dried up, not because he had done something wrong or because he wasn't holy or righteous enough, but simply because there was no rain.

There are things that you are going through right now that are beyond your control. In other words, it's not your fault. You can't control the rain. What we discovered is that when this

160

happens, God often opens up a world of possibilities on our behalf. Your greatest blessings come after your worst days, after you just feel like you are not going to make it, and you feel like giving up. That is when God steps in. I call it a holy setup. You are being set up by God, not by the enemy. Your enemy would not set you up like that, because he does not want your end to be better than your beginning. When God set you up, He is allowing you to go through the things you are going through just to get you to where you need to be. In the end, you are going to say it was worth it, because if it had not been for the Lord who was on your side, where would you be? Have confidence in God to let Him do what He needs to do as it relates to your life. Can you let God handle your life? You will not always understand what God is doing, but allow Him to do it.

It is a difficult position for anyone having to face, especially those of us who are of the household of faith. Because we walk by faith, we live by faith; we are used to naming and claiming. Yet, at some point in our lives, we will get into a position that I call, "a position of uncertainty." That is, when you don't know what to do. You are not sure if you should go or stay. You are in a situation in which you really do not have the answer. You want to go, but God is telling you to stay. You want to stay, but God is telling you to step out on faith. It's too much for you to handle. You have bills to pay. You can't take chances like that because you don't know if you can make it or not. That is where God wants you to be.

He wants you to be in a position in which your back is against the wall and you are seeking Him for an answer. God said He'd be there when you need Him. Have you ever been in that type of position? In your worst times, you did not know if you were up or down, whether to go or stay, to laugh, or cry. You would laugh, but you felt like crying, and you were crying so much until you had to laugh at how often you were crying! People around you thought you were going to lose your mind. They said that you may have come out of those other little skirmishes you had, but they don't think that you can overcome this problem because of its severity.

Some of you have Job friends: people who come to encourage you but end up discouraging you by the things they say. That's where God wants you to be. When you don't know what to do, and your back is against the wall, it's time to take the mask off. You may be laughing on the outside, but you are crying on the inside, all torn up, messed up from the inside out. You rejoice in church, smile at work, but cry at home. If others only knew that you did not know what to do, did not know how you were going to make it.

How are you going to stand against the enemy that has come against you? Your true nature is about to be revealed. You are in a place that God wants you to be, and God is going to bless you like never before! Have you ever stayed up pacing the floor at night? Got up the next morning, dried your tears, put your clothes on, and went to work. Your colleagues didn't know the hell you went through the night before. Your back was against the wall. Just know that in the midst of your breakdown, God is going to send a breakthrough.

Why do bad things happen to good people? It seems like the people who are trying to live a holy life experience more trouble than those who are not. It seems as if the enemy bothers them more than anyone else. Can you sense that in your life? There was a king of Judah named Jehoshaphat who was a righteous king. Jehoshaphat was a good king who came from an evil father, yet it seemed as if his father had more success than he had. That is, before God turned it around. God wanted Jehoshaphat to know that He had to take him *through* some things before He could take him *to* some things. He didn't know what God was up to because God could not tell him everything. Jehoshaphat's enemies conspired against him and the nation. Jehoshaphat's back was against the wall. All of his enemies were united together, and they called it a great company — a great multitude of people. Have you ever felt as if more than one person was against you and the demons from the pits of hell were living in your house as well as on your job? It seemed that way because the enemy was trying to destroy you. So, when you don't know what to do, what then will you do?

Judah gathered together to ask help of the Lord. The Apostle Paul writes, *"Having therefore obtained help of God, I continue unto this day, witnessing both to small and great, saying none other things than those which the prophets and Moses did say should come."* [1] David writes,

"I will lift up mine eyes unto the hills from whence cometh my help."[2] They went and got some other worshippers. Judah didn't go to the Benjaminites, but the others went to the house of Judah to hook up with other worshippers, figuring that they had to be going through something similar. Similarly, you should find some real confidants. You may have been confiding in the wrong people. Your married partner may not be your spiritual confidant. Sometimes you have to pray about them and leave them at the altar. You've got to surround yourself with people who believe in God and trust His Word. Don't surround yourselves with people who look at you as if you've lost your mind when you say hallelujah. You are in the wrong crowd. You must surround yourself with people who, when you call on the name of Jesus, will know that you have not lost your mind, because the name of the Lord is a strong tower.

When you don't know what to do, you need to know who to go to. Gather yourself together and fall on your knees and say, *"Father, I stretch my hands to thee. No other help I know. If thou withdraw thy hand from me, whither shall I go?"*[3] Don't be ashamed to let the world know that you need God in times of crises.

Chapter Twenty-Two

When You Don't Know Whom You Can Trust

Trust ye not in a friend, put ye not confidence in a guide: keep the doors of thy mouth from her that lieth in thy bosom. For the son dishonoureth the father, the daughter riseth up against her mother, the daughter in law against her mother in law; a man's enemies are the men of his own house. Therefore I will look unto the LORD; I will wait for the God of my salvation: my God will hear me.

Micah 7:5-7

Whom do you trust when you don't know whom to trust, when you have been abused and lied on by people who profess to be your friends? With friends like those, who needs enemies? Whom do you trust when you don't know whom you can tell your business to? There are times in your life when you have to know when to be quiet, when you can't tell anyone what you are going through. We have all been down that road before. Nothing hurts like being hurt by someone you least expected to hurt you. If you have lived long enough, you know what I mean. It feels as if people whom you trusted will often let you down. They will betray you more than you can imagine, but claim to be your friend. The one who said, "I have you covered," covered you so deep that you could not get up! It was the Judas kiss, which was not of affection, but of betrayal. When this happens, we should not become discouraged and give up.

Jonathan, the son of King Saul was a wonderful example of trust. He was loyal to David because David was his friend. *"But also thou shalt not cut off thy kindness from my house for ever: no, not when the LORD hath cut off the enemies of David every one from the face of the earth. So Jonathan made a covenant with the house of David, saying, Let the LORD even require it at the hand of David's enemies. And Jonathan caused David to swear again, because he loved him: for he loved him as he loved his own soul."* [1] You don't have a friend until they can love you like they love themselves. That is my definition of friendship. Do they love me as they love their own soul? Will they do for me as they will do for themselves? Until they can pass the Jonathan test, they may not deserve the title of friend. The greatest thing that Jonathan gave David was his future. Jonathan had every right to hate David and to despise him. Jonathan's father was King Saul, and Jonathan was in line to be the next king of Israel, not David. The position was Jonathan's because he was of the lineage of Saul; therefore, if anyone was going to have a problem with David, it should have been Jonathan.

That's why I love Jonathan, because Jonathan knew that it was not about him, his inheritance, or the kingdom because the kingdom wasn't his. Jonathan's loving David as he loved his own soul is a true definition of friendship. Have you ever had a friend stay by your side when you had nothing to give him, and when you couldn't do a thing for him but say "thank you"? I'm not talking about friends who love you as long as you have your material possessions. Job's friends stood by Job as long as he had his wealth, but when Job lost all of his possessions, he lost his friends. Don't call them friends until they have gone through some things with you. That is when you know that you have a friend. Otherwise, you have some "Job friends."

Job's so-called friends, Eliphaz, Bildad, and Zophar were trustworthy. Before Job lost his possessions, he was the talk of the town. Now he was the gossip of the town. He was at rock bottom. He was going through a difficult time. If he ever needed Eliphaz, Bildad, and Zophar, he needed them now. These were not young men. They knew Job.

"Now when Job's three friends heard of all this evil that was come upon him, they came every one from his own place; Eliphaz the Temanite, and Bildad the Shuhite, and Zophar the Naamathite: for they had made an appointment together to come to mourn with him and to comfort him. And when they lifted up their eyes afar off, and knew him not, they lifted up their voice, and wept; and they rent every one his mantle, and sprinkled dust upon their heads toward heaven. So they sat down with him upon the ground seven days and seven nights, and none spake a word unto him: for they saw that his grief was very great." [2]

They made an appointment to meet with Job. They sat down with Job for seven days and nights. When they finally opened their mouths to speak, Job wished they had kept their mouths shut. Job shows how you should label your acquaintances that are under the pretense of caring about you: *"Then Job answered and said, I have heard many such things: miserable comforters are ye all."* [3] Job calls them miserable comforters!

Have you ever had friends come to comfort you, and at the end of the day, have the audacity to tell you how bad off you are? It is usually the ones who talk the most who have nothing really to say. However, the people who say the least are the ones who will encourage you the most. Some of the people in your life are just taking up your time. You may have to change your circle of friends.

Eliphaz told Job that he was in the shape that he was in because he sinned. He advised Job to go to God. Eliphaz thought he had a Word from God. Job's response was for Eliphaz to stop assuming his guilt, because Job knew that he was righteous. You have to have a word for the naysayer in your life. Bildad also sat in silence for seven days, then told Job that his problem was that he was a sinner. They asked Job how long he would continue in denial. Job responded that he would ask God himself. The third friend, Zophar, told Job that his sin deserved more suffering than he was getting now. You see, there are some people who think that you should be worse off than you already are. They think that you don't have enough pain in your life. So-called friends sat with this man for seven days after he had lost everything, and they told him that he should be suffering more than he was suffering.

Thanks to God, Job knew he would be justified. He knew that he did not do anything wrong. He knew that he had not hurt anyone. Job's fourth friend, Elihub, told Job that he did not have anything to say. He just felt that God was using Job's suffering to mold him, to train him and to make him the man that God wanted. Perhaps what he was going through had a greater purpose. You see, the best advice came last. If you can go through the naysayer, God will send someone in your life with an encouraging word. Wait on the real thing. God will be your friend. Solomon says, *"Trust in the LORD with all thine heart; and lean not unto thine own understanding. In all thy ways acknowledge him, and he shall direct thy paths."* [4] Wait on a word from the Lord. God will send it to you. A true friend loves at all time.

You may have been wounded and hurt by people who said it was your fault or people who said if you would confess you would be okay, and still others who said that you deserved more than you got. There are some "haters" in all of our lives. Job's three friends had no good intentions. Deep down inside they probably rejoiced over Job's demise because somehow it made them feel or look better. There are people in your life who will rejoice over your demise, because they think it makes them look holier. The Lord turned the captivity of Job when Job prayed for his friends. Also, the Lord gave Job twice as much

169

as he had before. God allowed other people to bless Job. After they hurt and disappointed Job, God raised up new friends in Job's life. God is getting ready to expand your circle. He has to show you everyone who is not on your side. He has to expose the hypocrites to you so that you will know the real thing. You have so-called friends in your life who just want to take and not give. They are not your friends. We must learn to put our trust and confidence in the Lord, our one true friend.

CHAPTER TWENTY-THREE

When You Are Desperate for a Miracle

And they came to Jericho: and as he went out of Jericho with his disciples and a great number of people, blind Bartimaeus, the son of Timaeus, sat by the highway side begging. And when he heard that it was Jesus of Nazareth, he began to cry out, and say, Jesus, thou Son of David, have mercy on me. And many charged him that he should hold his peace: but he cried the more a great deal, Thou Son of David, have mercy on me. And Jesus stood still, and commanded him to be called. And they call the blind man, saying unto him, Be of good comfort, rise; he calleth thee. And he, casting away his garment, rose, and came to Jesus. And Jesus answered and said unto him, What wilt thou that I should do unto thee? The blind man said unto him, Lord, that I might receive my sight. And Jesus said unto him, Go thy way; thy faith hath made thee whole. And immediately he received his sight, and followed Jesus in the way.

Mark 10:46-52

There are two words that I need to define, as it brings into focus what this chapter is about: the word "desperate" and the word "miracle." The word *desperate* means, *"being almost beyond hope."* [1] This is close to giving up; down to your last dime; pink

171

slip on your kitchen table; phone already turned off; and your lights are next!

The word *miracle* is not a convenient thing that God can give you if He so desires. A miracle is defined as *"an extraordinary event manifesting divine intervention in human affairs."* [2] It's not what you can do, because if you could fix it, it's not a miracle. If you can figure it out, it is not a miracle. A miracle is what you cannot fix, what you cannot work out, what you cannot even touch. A miracle is not about upgrading from a Camry to a BMW. There are times in your life when you need a supernatural intervention from you divine Creator, times when you need a "right-now" blessing. You need God to step in the fire. If God doesn't do it, you will not make it.

Jericho was no ordinary city in Palestine during the days of Jesus. It was seventeen miles from Jerusalem. It was the commercial hub of that day. As Jocephus writes in his antiquities, everyone sooner or later traveled the Jericho Road. That is where they went to buy their goods and services. It was a very busy place. Outside of Jericho was the highway known as the Wayward Highway. Everyone who needed something hung out on that highway. That is where those who needed help would stand and beg.

According to Matthew Henry's commentary, men and women who had needs, such as the lame, blind and disabled, would stay on the Jericho Road. When someone on the Jericho Road recognized a person of means nearby, others would cry out to them, but if someone without means walked by, they remained quiet. They had been doing this all their lives. Those who were blind would wait until they heard others cry out, and then they would also cry out.

There was a man named Bartimaeus, the son of Timaeus, who was born blind. He sat on the Jericho Road. One of the advantages of being on the Jericho Road was that they heard all kinds of rumors. One of the rumors was that there was a Messiah that was born in Bethlehem. The rumor mill was working on the Jericho Road. One day, someone announced that Jesus from Nazareth was coming down the road. Although there were many blind people on the Jericho Road, Bartimaeus had heard that Jesus was passing by. He jumped up and cried out, "...*Jesus, thou son of David, have mercy on me.*" [3] Bartimaeus was told to be quiet, but he cried out all the more. Bartimaeus heard what others did not hear. He did what no one else on the Jericho Road did. Sometimes you have to look ridiculous to get a supernatural blessing. If you want what other people will not get, you've got to do what others will not do. Bartimaeus recognized that Jesus was more than the son of Joseph.

Bartimaeus knew that Jesus was no ordinary man. He recognized Jesus as a doctor in the sick room. Maybe they thought others wanted Bartimaeus to be quiet because people who were with Jesus might have had something to give, and they didn't want to lose possible blessings from the people who were around Jesus. Bartimaeus was desperate for a miracle. He cried all the more. Bartimaeus could not see, yet he had faith enough to speak into existence what he wanted. When you can't see your way, you must know that there is a way. There is a blessing with your name on it. Bartimaeus expected what others did not expect. Everyone else was looking for money. Bartimaeus asked to receive his sight. He expected a miracle. He cried out for a miracle. When you get your miracle, you should praise God for what He has done in your life. Perhaps there is a miracle getting ready to walk down your street.

If you cry out for it, you can have it. Look for a miracle. Expect the impossible. A world of possibilities awaits you.

CHAPTER TWENTY-FOUR

When You Just Have to Praise Him

And it was told King David, saying, The LORD hath blessed the house of Obededom, and all that pertaineth unto him, because of the ark of God. So David went and brought up the ark of God from the house of Obededom into the city of David with gladness. And it was so, that when they that bare the ark of the LORD had gone six paces, he sacrificed oxen and fatlings. And David danced before the LORD with all his might; and David was girded with a linen ephod. So David and all the house of Israel brought up the ark of the LORD with shouting, and with the sound of the trumpet...

2 Samuel 6:12-15

Have you ever felt that there were times in your life in which you had no choice *but* to praise God? Have you ever felt that you just had to praise God? There comes a time when you just have to praise Him.

This chapter does not deal with struggles or challenges, it deals with joy and delight, such as when you do something that you want to do or enjoy doing. We often do things that we are forced to do. Oftentimes in our daily lives, we are dealing with struggles and disappointments that seem to weigh us down.

It seems like every day, we have challenges and struggles, as if the enemy takes advantage of the occasion. He often uses this occasion to depress us or to weigh us down. The enemy knows how to whisper in our ears, saying, "Although you go to church, your brook has dried up. You paid your tithes, but you don't know how you are going to pay your rent." The adversary often steps in when we are most vulnerable, to discourage us from walking with the Lord. He drops his venomous messages in our ears and in our spirit.

He tries to turn us around. So now, we flip the script, turn the tables, and worship in the presence of our enemies. King David declared, *"Thou preparest a table before me in the presence of mine enemies."* [1] This is our chance to rejoice before the Lord and tell the enemy, "I told you so. I knew that God would keep His promise and do just what He said He would do." There are things that bring us great joy and make us smile when others are frowning. These are the times in which the saints of God put a skip in their step and say, "God is good all the time. All the time, God is good." Has God made a way for you such that He has earned the right for you to praise Him? When it looked as if all was hopeless and you thought you were going to lose your mind, God stepped in and made a way. God brought unspeakable joy to your life. How long has it been since you praised God? What would it take to make you lose your composure? What would it take to make you raise your hand in worship? You may not be comfortable doing this, but considering where He brought you from, you should change the manner of your praise. What does it take for you to give God your best praise?

We have an example of what it took for King David to lose his composure completely. He laid aside his royal regalia in order to praise God. It must have been something special that reminded King David of his past that made him give God this type of crazy praise. I'm not referring to cute praise in which we raise our silk handkerchiefs in the air; it's deeper than that! I'm talking about when you sit on the edge of your seat, and you are about to leap out of your skin, and God just reminded you of something He did for you!

It's realizing that you should still be locked up in prison, but God made a way for you. Do you have a crazy praise? You haven't always looked as good as you do now or dressed as nicely as you do now. You should give the highest praise you can. Because you have so much, you should praise God even more. When I think about how good God has been to me, it makes me want to praise Him. There is forgiveness in the presence of God. When He shows up, He casts our faults into the sea of forgetfulness and heals our infirmities. God gives us second chances because of His mercy.

For seventy years in the life of Israel, the Ark of the Covenant was missing. It had been taken by the Philistines for seven months. The Philistines recognized their doom in taking the Ark and now were trying to return the Ark because of the trouble and chaos it brought. *"And they sent messengers to the inhabitants of Kirjath-jearim, saying, The Philistines have brought again the ark of the Lord; come ye down, and fetch it up to you."* [2] So the men of Kiriath-jearim came to take the Ark of the Lord from the Philistines and carry it to the home of Abinadab where the Ark of the Covenant remained for twenty years, until King David transported the Ark of the Covenant to the home of Obededom of Gath. The Ark of the Covenant remained in the home of Obededom for three months, and the Lord blessed him and his household.[3]

The word went back that everything in Obededom's house was blessed because the presence of God was there. Obededom was one blessed man! Others inquired why this man was so blessed. King David was told that somewhere hidden in his house was the Ark of the Covenant. Because the presence of God does not discriminate, wherever He shows up, He blesses. Where God's presence is, everything around His presence is blessed. King David set out on a mission to go back and recover the presence of God. King David believed that one of his purposes in life was to restore the presence of God to the city of Jerusalem. He had a great passion for being in the presence of God. He did not just send men to get the Ark; he went with them. He was so happy and so overcome with joy that every six paces, he had to stop and give God a shout of praise. You should be able to stop every now and then before you get to where you are going and give God praise. When others on the job are taking a smoke break, you should give God a praise break! Every six paces, King David gave God a sacrifice and leaped for joy. As he entered into the city of Jerusalem his wife, the daughter of Saul, whom David succeeded, looked out her window and judged him.

There are people who don't want to go with you to get your blessings, but sit in their ivory towers and judge you over how you praise God. *"And David danced before the Lord with all his might."* [4] On his way back with the Ark, he gave God an intermediary praise, a praise that was good for the transition, but when he returned to the city, he danced before the Lord until his royal purple robe fell off in the streets. As with everything, you should know that not everyone celebrates your praise with you. Sometimes, the people who are closest to you will not celebrate. Saul's daughter could not imagine what David was going through on the inside. Unlike David, she never had to sleep in a cave. Michal grew up in royalty, whereas David grew up a shepherd boy, but he had something that she did not. He had a relationship with God. God wants you to humble yourselves so that he can speak to you. David had to get his wife straight. He had to remind her of his story. He had to remind her that God had elevated him above her father. God had given him positions he never imagined. God anointed his head with oil. God chose him, snatched him from tending sheep, and made him the King of a unified Israel. There was a reason David acted the way he did. He had to give God his best praise! God shut the womb of David's wife, and she bore no fruit because she criticized his praise.

Do not ever allow your circumstances to hinder your praise. Praise God in spite of your circumstances. Whatever you do, do not allow your position to hinder your praise. Do not allow people who don't know your story to hinder your praise. Don't allow people who don't know how far God has brought you to hinder your praise. Don't ever stop praising God. Bless God at all times.

CHAPTER TWENTY-FIVE

God Is Able to Give You More than You Ever Had Before

And it shall come to pass, if thou shalt hearken diligently unto the voice of the LORD thy God, to observe and to do all his commandments which I command thee this day, that the LORD thy God will set thee on high above all nations of the earth: And all these blessings shall come on thee, and overtake thee, if thou shalt hearken unto the voice of the LORD thy God. Blessed shalt thou be in the city, and blessed shalt thou be in the field. Blessed shall be the fruit of thy body, and the fruit of thy ground, and the fruit of thy cattle, the increase of thy kine, and the flocks of thy sheep. Blessed shall be thy basket and thy store. Blessed shalt thou be when thou comest in, and blessed shalt thou be when thou goest out...

Deuteronomy 28:1-6

God has made you a promise to open to you His treasure. If you live right and walk upright before God, He is going to do for you what only God can do. There will be others around you who will be filled with envy because they do not have what you have, simply because they do not have the relationship with God that you have. Increase — that is what God has promised. If you think you have something now, know that He is going to give you more. When you look at Job, people will conclude that it wasn't fair for Job to get twice as much as he had, because he already had more than others did. God does not grade on a curve. In other words, He won't bring you down in order to bring others up.

There are no limits to what you can do, and what you can have, and what God can do in your life. If you think that you are living well now, why can't God make you live better? If last year was the best financial year of your life, you haven't seen next year. God gives increase; however, there is a process. We all look at Job and look at what he started out with and what he ended up with, but there was a process that occurred between his beginning and his end. Consider these facts:

1. Job was blessed from the beginning. That did not hinder God from wanting to bless him more. There are those who think that because you are blessed, you should be content and not expect any more. Every round with God goes higher. If you expect on your earthly job cost-of-living raises, if your earthly providers can give you minimum increases just to keep up with inflation, why can't God add more to what you already have? It all depends on what you expect from God. I am convinced that the reason why some people cannot get an increase is because they can't deal with what they have. They get lifted up in pride, and God is holding them accountable for what they do with what they have. They can't handle

what God has given them. If you get the big head driving a Pontiac — which is a wonderful car — how are you going to handle a Mercedes? *"But as it is written, Eye hath not seen, nor ear heard, neither have entered into the heart of man, the things which God hath prepared for them that love Him."* Everything that you are asking God to prepare for you is already done. I get upset when people say that God is working on their blessing, as if God needs to do that. No. Your blessing has been completed, but he is working on you. God had some things prepared for Job from the beginning. God has the advantage of seeing the beginning and the end, so He looks down through infinite time, sees Job, and says if people hated Job in Chapter One, wait until they get to Chapter Forty-two. If you thought he was blessed then, wait until the end. If others are jealous now, they will not be able to stand it when God gets finished with you. That's their problem.

2. Job was blessed from the beginning, and through no fault of his own, he lost just about everything. He did not contribute to his own demise.

3. Job never lost his integrity. He never lost his faith. Can your integrity withstand your persecution? Can your faith withstand your valley experiences? When things go badly, does your faith go down? Job never lost his integrity or his faith. He still praised God. *"And the LORD said unto Satan, Hast thou considered my servant Job, that there is none like*

him in the earth, a perfect and an upright man, one that feareth God, and escheweth evil? and still he holdeth fast his integrity, although thou movedst me against him, to destroy him without cause." [2] In other words, Job went through the worst that one can go through, but he held fast to his integrity. If you lose your possessions, do not lose your integrity. You can get more stuff. As a matter of fact, you can get better stuff. If you can go through the process, God will give you more than you had before. Job held on to his faith and his integrity. *God forbid that I should justify you: till I die I will not remove mine integrity from me.* [3] Even though his friends came and falsely accused him, he would not change. Can you withstand persecution, trouble, and tribulation? Can you withstand people falsely accusing you? So many can lose houses and cars but cannot stand to lose a friend. Their faith will waver because of others' opinions and accusations, not Job.

4. God decided to turn it around for Job when he became selfless and not selfish. In other words, when you get enough faith, you can pray for those who sit at your house for three days, eat your food, and accuse you falsely. If you can turn around at those same people and pray that God would bless them, then you are headed in the right direction. Until you can pray for those who spitefully use you and those who have hurt you, your blessing will be held up because you can't forgive. Job

could have been angry with his friends, but he did not. He prayed for his friends.

Do you want increase? There is a process that leads to your increase. You must pray for those who have hurt you, even though you did not do anything to them. God had a blessing for Job since the beginning of time. And God blessed the latter end of Job more than his beginning.[4] Do you want increase? Write down these words, integrity, faith, and forgiveness. Put them into practice and watch God bless you. How did Job get his blessings? People for whom Job had no use were the ones who blessed Job. God has a blessing for you that the enemy paid for. *"...the wealth of the sinner is laid up for the just."* [5]

When God blesses people you know, don't become envious of what God is doing in their lives. You have to learn how to celebrate their blessings and wait on God to bless you. I could never understand why some people get jealous because God blesses someone else. What God does for others, He can do for you. Your increase is tied to your integrity and your faith. God is not going to give cheaters more. If you rob God with a $100- a-week job, why would God give you a $1,000-a-week job? God does not tie increase to the lack of integrity. God knows that when He blesses you, you will bless Him.

CHAPTER TWENTY-SIX

God Is Able to Take You Somewhere You've Never Been Before

But as it is written, Eye hath not seen, nor ear heard, neither have entered into the heart of man, the things which God hath prepared for them that love him.

1 Corinthians 2:9

For if thou altogether holdest thy peace at this time, then shall there enlargement and deliverance arise to the Jews from another place; but thou and thy father's house shall be destroyed: and who knoweth whether thou art come to the kingdom for such a time as this?

Esther 4:14

Get ready to relocate. Those who resist the move of God based upon the uncertainty of not knowing where they are going, miss out on the blessings of their lives. A whole lot of people are so cautious and conservative that they won't move unless they see their way. Faith is moving without seeing your way. Faith is moving without having been told where you may end up. God will show you as you go. He will do it as you step out.

God has something for you. You have to believe that God has blessings for you that no one knows about. Your friends can't bless you because they don't always know what you need. We often want people to bless us, but they are limited in their ability and their capacity to understand. There are those who, if they could bless you, they would. Then there are others who could bless you but won't. You probably know both.

Some people don't want anyone to be blessed but them and their family and their clique. They don't care about anyone else outside their clique and their universe. The good news is that they can't hinder your destiny. If gossip could stop destiny, a whole lot of people would be in trouble. I am so glad that envy, gossip, and hatefulness cannot control my destiny.

Favor is something God gives out. For every Esther and Mordecai, there is a Haman. But for every Haman, there is divine justice. You see, Esther's cousin Mordecai raised her. Mordecai worked in the palace of the king, yet Mordecai had nothing, whereas Haman had everything. Haman was a man of privilege, a man who had possessions. He was next in line to the king; he had all he could ask for. So, how is it that people can be jealous of you when you don't have anything? Mordecai was a Jew in captivity in Persia. He was a third-generation captive with nothing. Haman was a Persian leader, a man with privilege and possessions, and yet, he was jealous of Mordecai. Why? Because Haman's spirit knew something about Mordecai's spirit. There are those in your life who are jealous of you and don't know why. Perhaps they sense that God is getting ready to bless you. Some are jealous before they even have anything to be jealous over. Their jealousy still cannot stop your destiny. What God has destined for you cannot be denied. You should not worry about things you cannot control. Because what is yours is yours, and no one can take what God has for you.

Sometimes God allows the enemy to take things out of your life, knowing that He is going to make room for some better things. When Haman was elevated, everyone bowed down to him except Mordecai. Instead of saying, "Look at all these people honoring my promotion," Haman was upset because of the one who did not bow down. Mordecai had a reason not to bow down; he was true to his faith, which said, *"Thou shalt not bow to their gods."* [1] From that point on, Haman was out to destroy Mordecai and all Jews. Haman knew that he could not go after Mordecai alone, because Mordecai had favor. That is why he went after all the Jews. But God had another plan. What Haman did not know was that God knew from the beginning of time that there would be a Haman, and the evil he would have in his heart. That is why God birthed into this world an Esther, born to parents who would die and leave her alone. Esther was being raised by her cousin Mordecai, and that worked to her advantage. There are some things that you are going through now, and you despise the process, not knowing that the process could work to your benefit.

Haman built a noose and a platform in preparation for destroying Mordecai. Be careful whom you dig ditches and build platforms for. How do you know that the same thing that you build for someone else won't destroy you? In between Haman's plan and the execution, God was raising Esther up. Of all the people whom the king could have chosen, he chose Esther. The king had a party inviting all his people, and he invited his beautiful wife, Vashti, to show herself off to his friends, but she wouldn't do it. The king dethroned her. He took off her crown. In all accounts, we don't see where she did much wrong. What the king was asking her to do was pretty embarrassing, but it wasn't about her. What Vashti did not know was that she was part of the master plan. The scriptures never say that Vashti knew Esther. It wasn't that Esther took Vashti's position. God took it away from Vashti because it was Esther's time to shine.

See, it was the divine intervention, which allowed Mordecai to keep his position in the king's palace. Don't despise the little things God asks you to do. It may just get you in the place where you can get a blessing from God. God had Mordecai in the right place at the right time to hear the right word. When the word went out that the king was looking for a queen, he ran home and got Esther. *"And the king loved Esther above all the women, and she obtained grace and favour in his sight more than all the virgins; so that he set the royal crown upon her head, and made her queen instead of Vashti."* [2] Why Esther? She was a servant girl

189

in captivity. But when God gets ready to bless you, He will bless you despite your current circumstances. You don't have to worry about others setting you up to be in the right position, rubbing shoulders with the right people, wanting someone to introduce you to the right person; no, no, no. It doesn't work that way. If God be for you, who can be against you?

If you read the scripture, you will see that Esther obtained grace and favor in the King's sight more than all the virgins. It is important to note that they were all virgins. It wasn't as if Esther was the only virgin. They all had a stellar background. Don't look down on people because they are not chosen for what God has for you. You see, there are some people who are just as good, just as righteous as you are; yet God is going to pick you above them. *"Favor isn't fair."* I would rather have favor than position. When you have the favor of God, your enemy and your foe will stumble and fall when they come up against you.

Esther was sent there for a purpose. God will bless you, and when you get there, you've got to remember where you came from and those who helped you. You must reach back and help someone else. Don't become presumptuous and egotistical. Look at what happened to Haman. *"So they hanged Haman on the gallows that he had prepared for Mordecai. Then was the king's wrath pacified."* [3] *"And the king took off his ring, which he had taken from Haman, and gave it unto Mordecai. And Esther set Mordecai over the house of Haman."* [4] God will bless those who help others reach their destiny.

For every person who enjoys the blessings of God, there is a Haman nearby who hates you for no reason. Haman despised the whole nation of Jews. He had it in for Esther's cousin from the beginning. There are those who don't like you because they don't like someone who is close to you. There are those who will despise your blessings. God chose to bless you. You never bragged about it; you never made yourself out to be better than anyone else; you never threw it up in anyone's face. You just did what God asked you to do, and God blessed you. And just because of favor, people despise you. There may be those within your own family who want you to fall flat on your face. There are those among you who don't want you to succeed, but you have to see through it. As God said to Jehoshaphat in the book of Chronicles, you have no need to fight this fight. Not this time. Let God handle it. Your time is coming. When the favor of God is on you, God will destroy those who tried to destroy you. When you help someone who has the favor of God, God will bless you. What would happen if Mordecai despised Esther? He would not have received the favor of God. But he did what he felt was right by helping her with her blessing, and God gave favor unto him. Be a blessing to someone else, and watch how God pours blessings upon you. In the scripture, you will see that Esther, in turn, put Mordecai over the house of Haman. What God has for you is for you. He will take you somewhere you've never been before.

CHAPTER TWENTY-SEVEN

God Is Able to Make You Better than You Were Before

But as it is written, Eye hath not seen, nor ear heard, neither have entered into the heart of man, the things which God hath prepared for them that love him.

1 Corinthians 2:9

And his brethren also went and fell down before his face; and they said, Behold, we be thy servants. And Joseph said unto them, Fear not: for am I in the place of God? But as for you, ye thought evil against me; but God meant it unto good, to bring to pass, as it is this day, to save much people alive.

Genesis 50:18-20

So far, we have discussed God's unlimited possibilities for those who qualify. This is not for everyone. Some will do just enough to be saved, while others will be blessed beyond the gift of salvation. To those who qualify, these possibilities are yours: the blessing of Job, which is God's increase, the blessing of Queen Esther, which is God's favor. We will now look at the blessings of Joseph, which is when God intervenes on your behalf.

To intervene is *"to come in or to come between in order to stop, settle or to modify something that is already in the process of happening."* [1] Prevention is different. Prevention stops things from happening. There are times when your drama is already in progress. In that case, you don't need prevention because you cannot prevent something that is already in motion. It's too late. You need God to intervene. You need something or somebody to show up in the midst of it all to change what is going on. That is the blessing of Joseph. That is the blessing of when God intervenes.

There is a difference when God intervenes in your life. Your mother-in-law may intervene. Your cousins may intervene. But when God Himself steps in the midst of your life to stop, settle, or modify your situation that's special. Prevention for Shadrach, Meshach, and Abednego could have happened before they were put in the fire if God would have stepped in to stop them from going into the furnace. Many people wonder why God did not prevent some events from happening in their lives. There are different levels of blessings. If God prevented things from happening in your life, then perhaps you would not see the full manifestation of the power of God. For some, when God helps them to avoid situations, they take it lightly, not always realizing how bad it could have been.

When God intervenes in our situations, we are better off than we were before. Shadrach, Meshach, and Abednego were blessed young men, but when they came out of the fire, they were promoted over all of the providence of Babylon. If God had prevented the fire, they probably would not have gotten their promotion. One of the reasons you may be going through crises is because God is working on your promotion. You may be going through a midnight experience while God is working on your morning blessing.

Joseph enjoyed the favor of his father over his eleven brothers. Although he was not the oldest or the youngest, he was the favorite; he was favored of God. The text says, *"Now Jacob loved Joseph more than all his other children."* [2] It wasn't Joseph's fault. Don't you know that wherever there is favor, jealousy and envy can't be too far behind? The Bible says that jealousy is crueler than the grave. Joseph's brothers hated him. The text further says, *"And when his brethren saw that their father loved him more than all his brethren, they hated him, and could not speak peaceably unto him."* [3] There are those who are treating you badly simply because you are blessed by God. Whenever you get your blessing, expect the twin brothers of jealousy and envy to show up. Joseph's brothers dislike for him was not based on anything he had done but on who he was. Because he was the favorite son, they disliked him. The ironic thing about this text is that the ones that hated him the most were those who were closest to him.

The brothers of Joseph erroneously thought that they could undo God's favor. You cannot undo God's favor. If God's favor could be undone, then you would not be enjoying the blessings you enjoy right now. The brothers thought that hardship, trouble, and tribulations would undo the favor that Joseph enjoyed, but what they did not realize was that hardship and trouble and tribulation only gave him more favor. God's favor is not predicated on where you are. If you are favored by God, He is still going to bless you regardless of where you are. Joseph's brothers placed him in a pit. It was the intention of the brothers to leave him to die in the pit. Favor showed up in the presence of his brother, Judah, and Judah said to his brothers, "Let us not leave him here to die, let us sell him into slavery."[4] When the enemy thought that he would die in the pit, Judah saved him from the pit. Judah means "praise." While you were in the pit, praise saved you. If you learn how to praise God, He will lift you up out of a pit.

They raised Joseph from the pit and sold him to the Ishmaelites, who took him down into Egypt. While in Egypt, he met Potiphar, who took him to be his personal assistant. Potiphar had a lustful wife who desired Joseph, but he resisted her. When you are under God's favor, you will have some convictions. You will stand for something. Because Joseph resisted the urges of his master's wife, he was put in a prison. When you are favored, wherever you are, you will rise to the top. In the prison, Joseph became the top prisoner.

The baker and butler said that they would remember him, but they didn't. God still intervened on his behalf. The jailor favored Joseph. There are those who will bless you who don't even know your name. You may not have the credentials as others, but you will be favored. Joseph was remembered when the king needed an interpreter. The King summoned Joseph. Here comes God. When his enemy meant to do evil, God was working on his behalf. Joseph interpreted the king's dream, and was elevated to be second in command. He became the governor of Egypt: from the pit to the prison to the palace. Isn't that like God? Now, here was Joseph, sitting in authority, second in command of all of Egypt, and his eleven brothers were starving because there was a drought in the land of their habitation.

God had to drive them out of there because destiny had to be fulfilled. At seventeen years old, Joseph had prophesied about his brothers kneeling down before him. Now, according to history, Joseph was about thirty-nine years old. Twenty-two years has passed between the promise and the manifestation of Joseph's promise.

Are you in the process of waiting on your blessing? Wait on God. He has already issued the promise. Somewhere between the promise and the palace was a pit and a prison. Somewhere between your promise and the manifestation of your promise may be a pit and a prison. However, it will not destroy you. As a matter of fact, the pit and the dungeon may be part of your matriculation process that will take you from one level to another level. You needed to go through that to get what is coming. In fact, it took twenty-two years for Joseph to see the manifestation of his dream. Joseph's brothers knelt down before him, but he insisted that they get up. Joseph said, *"Fear not: for am I in the place of God?"*[5] Joseph told them that what they meant for evil, God meant for good.[6] What was meant to destroy you has made you better. Maybe if you had not gone through your troubles, you would not be strong enough to stand today.

Even when you did things your way, God intervened on your behalf. You tried to destroy yourself, but God showed up in the midst of your destruction and declared, "Not this time." Your children might have been dead, but because of your prayers, God showed up in the midst of their destruction and said, "Not this child." Has God intervened in your life? God is standing between evil and your destiny. He is intervening in your life right now. You should thank God for intervening on your behalf. Having gone through the trails and tribulations, you are better because God was with you all along.

CONCLUSION:

A World of Possibilities Awaits You

In his letter to the Corinthians, Paul reminds us all to stay focused on the finish line, not on the obstacles we encounter along the way. In order to capture the rewarding life of *A World of Possibilities* that awaits you, you must keep your eyes on the prize. This is accomplished by focusing on your God-given purpose and by living each day with an awareness of its eternal significance.

Life can be challenging as you encounter painful trials and inevitable disappointments along the way. But with your faith firmly rooted in God and your identity grounded in the purpose for which He created you, you can experience God's presence.

Whether you're already living with a sense of purpose or struggling to discover what your purpose is, I hope the powerful message contained in this book has inspired you to let go of all that has kept you from reaching your full potential in life. Let go of anger, fear of failure, limited thinking, and pride. Let go of all that stops you from taking risks. Put your faith in God and stay in His perfect will. Only then can you be sure of accomplishing your God-given purpose. The purpose of life for you, and me, is to serve God and bring Him worship and glory through all that we do.

It is my prayer that you will be forever changed as you come to understand that *A World of Possibilities* awaits you!

About the Author

Darrell Jackson, Sr., is the senior pastor of Bible Way Church of Atlas Road in Columbia, South Carolina.

As pastor, he has implemented many programs and economic projects in the community surrounding the Bible Way Church. During his ten years as pastor, the church has grown to more than 10,000 members.

In addition to his pastoral responsibilities, Jackson is an entrepreneur and a member of the South Carolina State Senate, representing the Twenty-first District of Richland County.

He has received numerous awards including the Outstanding Legislator Award from the South Carolina School Boards Association (1999), the Legislator of the Year Award from the South Carolina National Chapter of Social Workers (2000), honorary doctorate degrees from Richard Stockton College of New Jersey (2000), and Benedict College (2002).

He is a graduate of Benedict College and Columbia International Seminary.

Jackson resides in Hopkins, South Carolina with his wife, Willie Mae. They have two sons, Darrell Jr. and Antoine Joseph.

You may contact Pastor Jackson and the Bible Way Church of Atlas Road:

Bible Way Church of Atlas Road
2440 Atlas Road
Columbia, SC 29209
803.776.1238
www.bwcar.org

ENDNOTES

Foreword
[1] Philippians 4:13

Introduction

[1] Jack Canfield, Victor Hansen, and Les Hewitt, *The Power of Focus: How to Hit* Your Business, Personal and Financial Targets with Absolute Certainty (Deerfield Beach, Fla.: Health Communications, Inc.)
[2] Ephesians 3:20

Chapter One
From Purpose to Possibilities

[1] *Merriam-Webster's Collegiate Dictionary,* 10th ed. (Springfield, Mass.: Merriam-Webster, 1993), 968.
[2] See 1 John 4:18
[3] See Matthew 14:28-29
[4] See Matthew 14:31
[5] See Luke 22:57
[6] See Matthew 28:10
[7] See Hebrews 11:1
[8] See Revelation 3:8
[9] See Hebrews 11:6
[10] Quote DB, *http://www.quoteb.com/quotes/2316*
[11] See Revelation 3:16
[12] See 2 Chronicles 20:15

Chapter Two
Who Me? The People of Possibilities

[1] See Psalm 130:3
[2] See Hebrews 11:7
[3] See Exodus 4:11-12
[4] See Judges 6:15-16
[5] See Deuteronomy 28:2

Chapter Three
The Promises of Possibilities

[1] See Numbers 13:30
[2] See Revelation 3:8
[3] See 2 Corinthians 1:20
[4] See 2 Peter 1:4
[5] See Deuteronomy 28:1
[6] ibid.
[7] See Deuteronomy 28:1
[8] See 2 Corinthians 1:20
[9] See Isaiah 40:31
[10] See Deuteronomy 28:11
[11] See Malachi 3:10
[12] See Luke 12:17-20
[13] Tommy Tenney, *The God Chasers* (Shippensburg, PA., Destiny Image Publishers, Inc. 2001)
[14] See Luke 12:19

Chapter Four
The Enemies of Possibilities

[1] See Job 1:6
[2] See Job 1:7
[3] See Genesis 50:20
[4] See Luke 8:22
[5] See Mark 4:38
[6] See Hebrews 11:1
[7] See Mark 4:41
[8] See Mark 4:39

Chapter Five
Yes, It Can Happen to You!

[1] See Matthew 7:7
[2] See James 4:2
[3] See Numbers 13:1-2
[4] See Numbers 13:17-18
[5] See Numbers 13:2
[6] See Genesis 32:24-28

Chapter Six
Yes, We Can

[1] See Luke 4:8
[2] Les Hewitt, *Power of Focus*
[3] See Philippians 4:12, New Living Translation

Chapter Seven
No More Fear

[1] See Matthew 8:26
[2] See Job 14:1
[3] See 2 Corinthians 5:1
[4] Zig Ziglar, *See You at The Top* (Pelican Publishing Co., 2000)
[5] See 2 Timothy 1:7
[6] See Numbers 13:32-33
[7] See Psalms 51:10-11
[8] See 1 Samuel 17:29
[9] See 1 Samuel 13:37

Chapter Eight
To Know Him

[1] See 1 Corinthians 10:13
[2] See Hosea 4:6
[3] ibid.
[4] See Psalm 46:10
[5] See Daniel 11:32
[6] See Mark 4:35-41
[7] See Mark 4:39

Chapter Nine
Anger: An Enemy of Possibilities

[1] R. Famularo, *Child Maltreatment Histories Among Runaway and Delinquent Children* (Clinical Pediatrics, 1990), 713-718
[2] See Genesis 4:5-9
[3] See Matthew 5:22
[4] See Matthew 5:21
[5] See Psalm 31:22
[6] See 1 Peter 5:7

Chapter Ten
Limited Thinking: An Enemy of Possibilities

[1] See Numbers 13:31
[2] See Ephesians 6:12
[3] See Numbers 13:33
[4] John C. Maxwell, *Thinking for a Change* (Warner Books, Inc., 2003), 13
[5] See Philippians 4:8
[6] See Hebrews 11:1
[7] See Hebrews 11:6
[8] See Philippians 4:13
[9] See Romans 8:28
[10] See Philippians 4:19

Chapter Eleven
Pride: An Enemy of Possibilities

[1] See Proverbs 6:7
[2] See Proverbs 16:18
[3] See Galatians 6:3
[4] William Shakespeare, *Hamlet. Act i. Sc. 3*
[5] See Proverbs 27:2
[6] See Proverbs 28:25-26

Chapter Twelve
The Spirit of Religion: An Enemy of Possibilities

[1] See Amos 5:21
[2] See Amos 5:23
[3] See 2 Timothy 3:4
[4] C. Peter Wagner, *The Second Apostolic Age: How God is Leading His Church into the Future* (Regal Books, 2004)
[5] See Luke 11:37

Chapter Thirteen
Blessings and Curses

[1] See Revelation 3:8
[2] See John 8:11
[3] See Deuteronomy 28:21
[4] See Deuteronomy 28:25

[5] See Deuteronomy 28:49-50
[6] See Deuteronomy 28:48
[7] See Deuteronomy 28:48
[8] See Psalm 17:8

Chapter Fourteen
Your Failures Have Not Ruined Your Possibilities

[1] *Merriam-Webster's Collegiate Dictionary*, 10th ed. (Springfield, Mass.: Merriam-Webster, 1993), 1069
[2] See Proverbs 23:
[3] See Philippians 2:5
[4] See Romans 12:2
[5] John C. Maxwell, *Failing Forward: How to Make the Most of Your Mistakes.* (Thomas Nelson Publishers, 2000)

Chapter Fifteen
Will You Believe What You Cannot See?

[1] See Hebrews 11:6
[2] See Numbers 3:19
[3] See Hebrews 11:1
[4] See John 20:28

Chapter Sixteen
Will You Go Where You Have Not Been?

[1] See Genesis 12:1-4
[2] See Proverbs 3:5-6

Chapter Seventeen
Will You Speak What You Cannot Prove?

[1] See Matthew 21:21
[2] See Acts 3:6
[3] See Job 42:11

Chapter Eighteen
Will You Sing Your Song in a Strange Land?

[1] See Mark 9:5
[2] See Psalm 137:4

Chapter Nineteen
The Power in You

[1] See Mark 9:5
[2] See Psalm 23:5
[3] See Philippians 2:5

Chapter Twenty
When the Brook Dries Up

[1] See Job 1:1
[2] See 1 Corinthians 10:13
[3] ibid.
[4] See Psalm 23:4

Chapter Twenty-One
When You Don't Know What to Do

[1] See Acts 26:22
[2] See Psalm 121:1
[3] Charles Wesley, A Collection of Psalms and Hymns, 1741

Chapter Twenty-Two
When You Don't Know Whom You Can Trust

[1] See 1 Samuel 20:15-17
[2] See Job 2:11-13
[3] See Job 16:1-2
[4] See Proverbs 3:5-6

Chapter Twenty-Three
When You Are Desperate for a Miracle
[1] *Merriam-Webster's Collegiate Dictionary*, 10th ed. (Springfield, Mass.: Merriam-Webster, 1993), 338

[2] *Merriam-Webster's Collegiate Dictionary,* 10th ed. (Springfield, Mass.: Merriam-Webster, 1993), 792

[3] See Mark 11:47

Chapter Twenty-Four
When You Just Have to Praise Him

[1] See Psalm 23:5

[2] See 1 Samuel 6:21

[3] See 2 Samuel 6:10-11

[4] See 2 Samuel 6:14

Chapter Twenty-Five
God Is Able to Give You More than You Ever Had Before

[1] See 1 Corinthians 2:9

[2] See Job 2:3

[3] Scc Job 27:5

[4] See Job 42:12

[5] See Proverbs 13:22

Chapter Twenty-Six
God is Able to Take You Somewhere You've Never Been Before

[1] See Exodus 23:24

[2] See Esther 23:24

[3] See Esther 7:10

[4] See Esther 8:2

Chapter Twenty-Seven
God is Able to Make You Better than You Were Before

[1] *Merriam-Webster's Collegiate Dictionary,* 10th ed. (Springfield, Mass.: Merriam-Webster, 1993), 655

[2] See Genesis 37:3

[3] See Genesis 37:4

[4] See Genesis 37:27

[5] See Genesis 50:19

[6] See Genesis 50:20